Countdown to College:

21 'To-Do' Lists for High School

Step-by-step strategies for 9th, 10th, 11th and 12th graders

Valerie Pierce, M.Ed., LPC,
and
Cheryl Rilly

4th Edition

Front Porch Press

Lansing, Michigan

www.frontporchpress.com

Countdown to College: 21 'To-Do' Lists for High School

Written by Valerie Pierce and Cheryl Rilly with Suzette Tyler
Page design by Terri Haas-Wittmann, Cheryl Rilly and Kelly McCarthy

Some quotes have been edited for clarity and brevity.

Published by Front Porch Press, 4733 Hawk Hallow Dr., Bath, MI 48808. Phone (517) 641-4489, Fax (517) 641-8408, E-mail: styler@frontporch-press.com

ISBN 978-0-9656086-6-4

Printed in The United States of America

Fourth Edition

acknowledgements
A special thank you to:

▷ **My daughter, Ashlie**, at the University of Texas, whose high school journey to a competitive college, forced me to create the original lists.

▷ **My husband David and son Tyler**, who still love and support me, after hearing about this book night and day for the last two years.

▷ **Renee Davis**, who encouraged me to use my lists to help other high school college bound students.

▷ **My original manuscript critics**: Carmen, Hayley and Sharon.

▷ **Mary Blaschke**, my daughters' high school counselor, who never appeared to tire from my questions.

▷ **Cy-Springs parents and faculty** who shared this high school journey.

▷ **Wilson and Watkins parents** who requested my original lists and now spread the value of these 'to do lists' to others.

▷ **To my family and friends** for understanding my passion about this book.

a special acknowledgement...

The heart and soul of this book belongs to the remarkable students who shared their thoughts, feelings and insights. Thanks everyone! It wouldn' t have happened without you!

Alexa Saiz, Alison Armstrong, Allison Sudol, Amanda Day, Amber Farris, Amy Meece, Ashlie Pierce, Becca Hall, Bonnie Plott, Brooke Clinton, Cassie Lawin, Catherine Osterman, Chris McMurtry, Clayton Farris, Courtney Chayes, Courtney Kurdziel, Diana Chan, Elizabeth Roman, Erica Kraus, Erika Sjoerdsma, Erin Sprague, Erin Weber, Eugenie Flash, Eva Davison, Fakhri Kalolwala, Garrick Malone, Holly Davidson, Jackie Forinash, Jamie Arredondo, Jason Midgett. Jenna Johansson, Jenni Manion, Jennifer Hassig, Jessica Shepherd, Jill Goodwin, John Holden, Jonathon Koller, Jordan Black, Joyce Jauer, Julie Calvert, Julie Christ, Justice Hampton, Kara Johnson, Kate Hansen, Katherine Schneider, Katie Rhodes, Katrina Bielawski, Ladd Williams, Lindsey Kallsen, Marcus Williams, Marie Falcone, Mary Steffel, Matt Japinga, Matt Klepac, Meaghan Casey, Meghan Miller, Melissa Bohlig, Melissa Lowery, Nicole Mitchell, Niesha Small, Philip Wells, Rebekah Hendrix, Robbie Simon, Robyn Gomez, Roohy Gupta, Sara Waterman, Sarah Dicello, Sheryl Franknecht, Siobhan Malone, Steve Song, Tania Yusaf, Tapas Nuwal, Tiffany Clark, Virginia Smith and William Solomon

Also a special note of gratitude to Jessica Rilly who became our high school freshman guinea pig. Thanks Jess!

table of contents

foreword

The race to the finish line—college, that is—began without our knowledge— when my daughter, Ashlie, entered the 9th grade. From the beginning our biggest problem was knowing what needed to be done before the deadlines passed. Ashlie's extra-curricular commitments, club meetings during homeroom, and trips to the orthodontist caused her to miss information on class meetings and deadlines. More often than not, I'd find student bulletins and parent meeting announcements in the backseat of the car, the floor of her bedroom, or in the trash pile of papers on the kitchen counter.

It didn't get better. Ashlie's activities increased: driver's ed, community service, SAT and ACT testing, evening high school and sports activities, and, oh, yes, schoolwork. To add to the confusion, there was a sudden onslaught of product information and college prep services all touting their own must-do-now importance. The only way out was to organize and prioritize. We made checklists for everything! It was the only way to get things done.

Those checklists became the basis of this book. Thanks to the help of my co-author, Cheryl Rilly, those lists have been expanded. We've gathered all the information, web sites, references, and resources you'll need for your own journey to college—and most importantly, a time-line you'll need to get things done.

Our many 'guiding lights' were the high school counselors and college admissions officers who so unselfishly lent us their expertise, wisdom and insider know-how. With that, many thanks to high school counselors Mary Blaschke, Mary Vertrees, John Dunn, Joanna Erdos, and Maggie Miller and to John Barnhill, Director of Admissions, Florida State University, Gordon Stanley, Director of Admissions, Michigan State University, Tim Washburn, Executive Director Admissions and Records, University of Washington, Dr. Frank Ashley III, Director of Admissions, Texas A&M University, David Drushcel, admissions counselor, Mt. Saint Clare College, and Jean Jordan, Admissions Officer, Emory University. And a special thanks to Suzette Tyler, our publisher and former academic advisor, Michigan State University.

Our other 'couldn't-have-done-it-without-them' group are the wonderful high school and college students who shared their experiences, regrets, and successes with us. You'll find their words throughout the book and a list of their names in special acknowledgements.

Whether you're an incoming freshman or a senior on the brink of making those all-important decisions, it's never too early or too late to use the tools in this book to enhance your high school-to-college experience. Just take it one step at a time.

Good Luck!

Valerie Pierce

Editor's Note: Since the original publication of this book, Valerie Pierce has received her M.Ed, LPC, and is currently counseling students in a Title 1 high school in Houston, Texas.

> **"** College? I barely knew
> my locker combination
> in the ninth grade. **"**

Freshman, Southwest Texas U.

freshman year
the journey begins

Even if you have no idea where or whether you want to go to college four years from now, the last thing you want is to find out as a senior that you messed up your chances . . . that there were things you could've done along the way that would've made you a 'shoe-in' at the college of your choice. So, not only should you be **thinking** about college, this book tells you what you can be **doing.**

College or not, the next four years are a chance for you to learn a little more about yourself: to try new things, to learn from mistakes, to dream . . . and to open doors.

66 The good thing
about being a freshman is
all of your choices
are in front of you . . .
you just have to
make the right ones. 99

High School Counselor

 freshman year

☐ **GO!** Before school starts, high schools have some type of orientation or open house for freshmen. It's your opportunity to ease into the next 4 years by learning about your school . . . or just find your locker.

☐ **Use it!** Your school's website can include all kinds of useful information and opportunities—graduation requirements, course descriptions, upcoming events, club activities, vacation days, college fairs, scholarships, job listings. It's a great resource for you and your parents.

☐ **Get connected** to your school's online information system and download suggested apps so you will receive notifications, teacher messages, assignments, academic support or whatever.

☐ **Get to know** teachers so they get to know you. At some point you may need recommendations for summer programs, scholarships and college applications. Watered down, generalized recommendations don't help much.

☐ **Visit** your school's college and career center. Check often for new information about workshops and scholarship opportunities. Know what dates representatives from trade and technical schools, colleges and universities, or the armed services will be at your school to talk with students.

A

❑ **Create** a file to keep all your important papers, grades, internet articles, scholarship opportunities or whatever.

❑ **Begin** your scholarship search, or at least, find out what kinds of things you'll want to be able to put on your application in a couple of years. (page 19)

❑ **Start** a log/journal/portfolio so you can keep track of your activities, volunteer work, jobs, and who the contact person is. Write down your impressions, especially what you do and don't like about each activity. Gradually, you may begin to see where your interests—and college major—lie. (page16)

❑ **Bookmark it.** *College Navigator* provides everything you want to know about 7,000 two-four year colleges—average test scores, majors, admission deadlines, campus events . . . it's all there.

nces.ed.gov/collegenavigator

66 I won the school Biology Award
and had become really excited
about medicine rather than engineering . . .
BUT I guess I never bothered to tell my
counselor that so he never bothered to tell me
about a program where high school seniors
are GUARANTEED
admission to medical school.
I don't even like to THINK about it . . . 99

Senior, Michigan State U.

let 'em know
who you are . . .

All kinds of cool stuff comes across high school counselors's desks—awards, contests, scholarships, special programs, leadership opportunities, camps . . . **Any one of them could have your name on it** if your counselor has gotten to know you and what your interests and goals are. *It's up to you to make sure he or she does.*

You'll also want to make sure your counselor recognizes why you are a good candidate for the college of your choice. If an admissions officer calls to discuss your application—often the case in borderline situations—your counselor needs to be as convinced as you are that you're a 'good fit'.

mapping out
your 4-year plan

Recommended courses for college:
(Check the course requirements for your 'dream' colleges and also any majors you're considering. Will your 4-year plan prepare you? Which math, which science or social studies, and which electives will do that best?)

English: 4 years

Science: 3-4 years with labs

Math: 3-4 years (4 years preferred)

Social Studies: 3-4 years

Foreign Language: 2-3 years in one language

Fine/performing arts: 1-2 years

Electives: Select courses that you're really interested in or related to a career you might like to explore. Strengthen your computer skills. If you are interested in AP classes or Dual Credit courses, allow for that in your course plan.

are 'honors' courses for you? It depends...

What type of college do you want to attend? Many selective schools give Honors and Advance Placement (AP) grades more weight because they want students who are willing to challenge themselves. So, a 3.5 in Honors English is worth more than a 4.0 in a regular class. The Top 50 Colleges expect you to do the maximum amount of work available to you.

On the other hand, there are many less selective schools that don't even take note of honors courses.

What kind of student are you? You DO want to challenge yourself in the courses in which you're strong, BUT you don't want to bury yourself or your GPA. If you think you can get a reasonable grade and you're excited about the coursework or the teacher, go for it.

66 I NEVER should've dropped
French my senior year!
I totally blew the college placement test...
I'd forgotten everything! **99**

Junior, U. of Georgia

timing IS everything

Set up your schedule so that your senior year includes the courses you'll need to continue as a college freshman. For example, if you're taking 3 years of a language, start in your sophomore year so you'll be 'fresh' for college language courses, or even test out of them altogether.

As for math, take all 4 years even if it doesn't 'agree' with you. That may be all you need to meet basic college requirements and/or you'll be better prepared to 'test out' of it. It's easier to 'gut it out' in high school than in college . . . ask any college freshman.

what colleges are looking for . . .

(ranked by importance)

1. GPA/Class Rank

2. SAT/ACT score

3. Extracurricular activities

Your essays

Teacher/counselor recommendations

...all of a sudden I'm in college
and need to pick up a major.
I wish I'd been more
'involved' in high school
...or worked or done something
that maybe would've given me
an idea of what I like,
what I'm good at...
It's scary not to know. 99

Freshman, Arizona State U.

it's all about you

you . . . who?

What do you like? If you could do anything, become anything, what would it be? Sure, high school is about learning and preparing for college, but it's also a time to find out about yourself—to become your own person, to think your own thoughts. To do that, you have to draw on your experiences. But, first you have to get them. The more experiences you have and the more you try different things, the more you'll know about yourself.

that's interesting . . .

Colleges want a well-rounded student who's interested and interesting. So, get involved. As a freshman, try a little of everything. As a sophomore and junior, concentrate on 2 or 3 things you really enjoy. That allows you to grow from a member (a joiner), to sitting on a committee (a team player), to heading a committee or holding office (a leader). It also gives the college an idea of what you'll do when you're on campus.

> 66 College admissions people are on the lookout for "clubbers"—people who join but don't do. . . 99

Admissions Guru,
www.mycollegeguide.org

> 66 I tried to do it all: student council, sports, drama, clubs, music. I finally realized that being interested in just a few things is more rewarding. Give your time to things you really love to do—not what you think you have to do. 99

Freshman, George Washington U.

it's all about you

☐ **Be a sport.** Try team sports or start a running club. Join a yoga class. Too strenuous? Join the pep club or ask the coach if you can film games, manage equipment, or be a student trainer.

☐ **Join a club** or start a club—whether it's academic (science, computers) or professional (Future Teachers, Junior Achievement) or social (chess, euchre). Participate in competitions and fairs.

☐ **Go political.** Run for student government or work on someone's campaign. Find a cause that interests you and collect signatures for a petition. Help raise funds. Join the debate team.

☐ **Work** on the school newspaper, the yearbook, or the school web site. Be a writer, photographer or even a webmaster!

☐ **Lend a hand.** Help with school activities, work on fundraisers, build floats, decorate for dances, or plan events.

☐ **Get cultured!** Join the band or choir. Act in a school play or join a community theater group. Can't act? Paint scenery, sell tickets, be an usher. Write poetry and post it online. There are some great sites to share your work and some offer free copyrights.

11

☐ **Travel** - long trips, short trips, day trips - every chance you get (page 80).

☐ **Volunteer.** Find a great position (page 13).

☐ **Get a hobby.** Check out hobby shops, craft stores and the internet for something interesting. Already have one? Search the internet for related organizations and activities.

☐ **Find a pursuit.** What's special about your heritage or where you live that makes you want to know more?

☐ **Set a goal.** Train for an event. Learn a new instrument. Audition for a play, a band, a commercial! Get certified as a lifeguard.

why volunteer?

a.k.a. 'chalking up points'

Okay, so maybe it *is* because you're such a caring person and not that your high school has a community service requirement or you need N.H.S. points. But don't pat yourself on the back too hard because chances are you'll get as much—or more —out of volunteering as the people you're helping. Not only will admissions folks be impressed but it's one more way for you to learn about YOU— what you do and don't enjoy, what you're good at, and maybe even what you'd like to do some day. Nothing beats a close-up look at what a job involves or meeting people who may be good contacts later. You may even get a lead on scholarships, a summer job, or an internship—not to mention, add to your people skills.

help yourself . . .

Find a volunteer activity that interests you and while you're there, check out the career possibilities. Or, work backwards. Got an idea of what career you'd like to have? Get a volunteer position in a related area. Then talk to people who have the job you want. Look around and find out if you'd be happy. For instance,

If you like: **Then:**

Architecture: → Build a house with Habitat for Humanity.

Forestry: → Be a guide at a state park.

Social Work: → Work at a soup kitchen.

Vet Medicine: → Help out at an animal shelter.

Ecology: → Work at a wildlife sanctuary.

Medicine: → Hospitals always need volunteers. Call one.

Music: → Work for a radio station's charity event.

Education: → Help with an after school program.

Computers: → Set up e-mail accounts for seniors in retirement centers.

History: → Be a museum guide.

Political Science: → Work on a campaign or cause.

Law: → Serve at a legal aid center.

Math: → Tutor younger kids in your school district.

. . . build your network

You'll meet a lot of people, many of whom you may be able to use as contacts in the admissions process and throughout life.

Keep a contact list that includes names, phone numbers, and email addresses.

www.volunteer

Help plant a memorial garden, read to the blind, work on a hotline, do crafts with kids, raise funds, tutor younger kids, collect toys for Christmas. Find opportunities like these and more in your own state at the following sites. They offer a variety of experiences and even tell you how to start your own volunteer program.

www.idealist.org
www.volunteermatch.org
www.1-800-volunteer.org
www.yudabands.org

the back door . . .

The Back-Door Guide To Short-Term Job Adventures by Michael Landes is a great source for volunteer work, internships, and summer jobs. Read the book and check out the web site for tips and updates:

www.backdoorjobs.com

go global

Any volunteer work you're doing locally can be done nationally or worldwide. In your junior and senior years, instead of working at a local park, contact the U.S. Forest Service and volunteer at a national park. Future architects can contact the U.S. Army Corp of Engineers. Summer programs worldwide need budding social workers. Contact your place of worship for missionary work that can take you into your own backyard or to another country. Many organizations are happy to pick up your expenses in exchange for your helping hand (**Travel,** page 82).

'quickies' that count

'Event volunteering' and 'virtual volunteering' are two ways to get in your service hours if time or transportation is a problem. Your services are required for a one day event or done via computer. For a schedule of volunteer events and virtual opportunities go to:

www.networkforgood.org/volunteer/

www.virtualvolunteer.org

log and learn

Your hours and efforts won't count towards any requirement, unless you document them. Make sure you get verification of your activities from the volunteer organization. Or, make your own log. Along with your name, the contact person's name and telephone number, the date, the activity and how many hours you spent, leave room to write what you liked and what you didn't like. Ask yourself these questions and include your thoughts:

- **What did I learn?**

- **What impressed me or suprised me the most?**

- **What was a total turn off?**

- **Did the activity leave me feeling good? Overwhelmed? Disinterested?**

- **What careers did I find out about?**

- **Do I want to learn more about it?**

- **Could I imagine doing this kind of work for life?**

volunteering

❏ **List** your interests and match them to possible service opportunities.

❏ **Call** professional organizations and associations related to your interests to see if they need volunteers or could suggest a volunteer position.

❏ **Click on** the web sites (page 15) for ideas. In your junior and senior years, check the sites for out-of-state opportunities.

❏ **Check** the school bulletin board or with your counselor to see what service possibilities exist through your school.

❏ **Ask** your friends where they plan to volunteer.

❏ **Check** the web sites of local newspapers and televison station for lists of volunteer activites and events. Watch for stories on interesting charity events. Call the sponsoring agency and ask if you can volunteer.

❏ **Call** the local sports teams to see if they're sponsoring youth events. Ask if you can volunteer.

❏ **Check** with your place of worship. Can you teach Sunday school?   Baby sit? Volunteer at church events?   Do they sponsor missionary work?

☐ **Turn** your interests into volunteer work. If you take extracurricular classes (i.e. dance, music), ask if they need help.

☐ **Start** your own volunteer group - form a 'zoo crew,' adopt a highway mile or adapt a program to suit your community.

TO HELP YOURSELF . . .

☐ **Be curious.** Find out what careers are related to the volunteer situation (i.e. hospital: doctor, nurse, radiologist, physical therapist, etc).

☐ **Talk** to your supervisor. Find out if your volunteer position can turn into a summer job or internship. Ask if he/she knows any programs or scholarships that could benefit you.

☐ **Use** your summer volunteer work to travel. Check with your place of worship for mission trips. Call the national headquarters of local organizations for out-of-state possibilities. Check the volunteer web sites for national or worldwide opportunities.

☐ **Create** a volunteer log or form letter to document your hours. Attach notes to your log about what you liked or disliked about a volunteer experience.

☐ **Ask** your counselor if your school has a program that gives high school credit for community service hours.

get

scholarships

you don't have to be Einstein . . .

. . . or a jock to get scholarships, but you do have to be detective. Finding scholarships is like a game of 'Where's Waldo?' There are scholarships for everything—bagpipe players, people under four feet tall, anyone who wants to study parapsychology or young women who want to become engineers. Start looking now because **it takes time!** Besides, it 'pays' to plan ahead. Some clubs and volunteer organizations give scholarships to members and workers. So, why not put your community service hours and extra-curricular time into an organization that ultimately may help you?

MY MAMA'S A TRUCK DRIVER

Great! Then she's probably a union member and most unions offer scholarships to family members. What you and your family do, where they work and shop all point to scholarship money. Check out this profile and then create your own. Include aunts, uncles, grandparents, cousins—the companies they work for and organizations they belong to. Then dig up your ancestors. What's your heritage? Ethnicity? Write down everything that makes you YOU.

Joe's scholarship leads include:

Businesses:
Coca-Cola
Wheaties
Doublemint
Tylenol
Calgon
Wal-Mart
Target
McDonald's
Exxon
Mastercard & Visa

Associations:
Naval Reserve
Lion's Club
Eagle Scouts
Luthern Brotherhood
Junior Achievement
Electricians union
Engineering society
Teachers' association

Contests:
Intel Science Talent Search
Baush & Lomb Science Award

Miscellaneous:
National Merit Scholarship
Texas A & M scholarships for sports, music, etc.
Sam Walton Community Scholarship
Polish/Slavic-related organizations

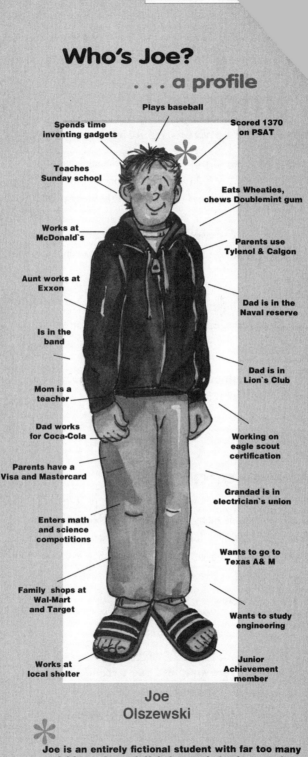

Who's Joe?
. . . a profile

Plays baseball

Spends time inventing gadgets

Scored 1370 on PSAT

Teaches Sunday school

Eats Wheaties, chews Doublemint gum

Works at McDonald's

Parents use Tylenol & Calgon

Aunt works at Exxon

Dad is in the Naval reserve

Is in the band

Dad is in Lion's Club

Mom is a teacher

Dad works for Coca-Cola

Working on eagle scout certification

Parents have a Visa and Mastercard

Grandad is in electrician's union

Enters math and science competitions

Wants to go to Texas A&M

Family shops at Wal-Mart and Target

Wants to study engineering

Works at local shelter

Junior Achievement member

Joe
Olszewski

Joe is an entirely fictional student with far too many activities to be real. He's here only to show you how many possibilities exist. No one expects you to be 'super student'. Do not try this at home.

...the

...ey!

Start your scholarship search at:

- **Libraries and bookstores.** Books such as College Board Scholarship Handbook come with a CD-ROM so you can view them via computer.

- **Your high school's college and career center** has scholarship books and may even have a scholarship database.

- **Your counselor** knows about many local scholarships. Show him/her the profile you've written and he/she may be able to suggest more.

- **Local businesses and organizations.** Call and ask if they sponsor scholarships, awards, or contests.

And . . .

the e-search

Scholarship search web sites speed up your research. Register with as many as possible and choose the broadest criteria for the most leads. The information will overlap but each site has one or two different listings that may be worth it.

www.finaid.org

www.fastweb.com

www.collegeboard.com

www.scholarships.com

www.princtonreviewcom/

www.xap.com

www.allaboutcollege.com

www.collegeview.com

www.unigo.com/scholarships

> **66** Senior year is the time to APPLY for scholarships, not LOOK for them . . . You don't have time! **99**

Sophomore, U. of Texas

In 10th, 11th and 12th grade

update your Internet searches and scan the books again. Check with the guidance office for any leads on local and national scholarships. Talk to seniors and find out what scholarships they qualified for, especially local scholarships.

When you start getting serious about what colleges are in the running, check out their web sites for scholarships available through them. Talk to the Financial Aid Officer and ask for leads. If you know what your major will be, call the departments at the colleges and ask if they know of any scholarships.

Get good at looking for scholarships. Once you're in college, there are more you can apply for every year—especially in your major.

never pay anyone to search for scholarships for you . . .

They'll only take the same information, plug it into the same sites and get the same results.

For information on scholarship scams go to:

www.fraud.org

www.finaid.org/scholarships/scams.phtml

it's never too early to hear
ka-ching!

Don't wait until you're a senior to cash in.
There's money available as early as your freshman year.
In addition to scholarships, there are CONTESTS! Even
if you don't enter anything as a freshman, knowing what's
out there now will help you decide what to go after later.
The list below will give you an idea of what's out there
starting in the 9th grade.

Contest	Award
American Legion Oratorical Contest	$1,500 - $18,000
Ayn Rand Essay Contests	$1,000
Burger King Scholars Program	$50,000
The DuPont Challenge	$50 - $1,500
Footlocker Foundation	$20,000
Google Global Science Fair	$50,000
National History Day Contest	$250 - $1,000
National Peace Essay Contest	$1,000 - $10,000
Prudential Spirit of Community Awards	$1,000 - $5,000
Scholastic Art and Writing Awards	$100 - $1,000
Toshiba/NSTA ExploraVision Awards	$100 - $10,000
Young Naturalist Awards	$1,000
Young America Creative Patriotic Art Awards	$500 - $3,000

*Information compiled from: **How To Go To College Almost For Free**,
Ben Kaplan.*

. . . mining for money

How To Go To College Almost For Free

Is an 'oldie but goodie' by Ben Kaplan, a one-
time public school student who wanted to attend
Harvard. His problem: no money. His solution:
scholarships, nearly $90,000 worth. He put his
tips and strategies into the book, a MUST read.

scholarships

YEARLY TO-DO'S:

☐ **First things first**—start a file for scholarships, awards, and contests. Keep adding and updating it yearly.

☐ **Search the sites.** Register at the web sites (page 22). Update your listing at least yearly or when your GPA and class rank change.

☐ **Check** out the scholarship section at the library and bookstores.

☐ **Enter** contests. Ask your counselor and teachers what programs they know of and check out : *The Ultimate Scholarship Book 2019: Billions of Dollars in Scholarships, Grants, and Prizes by Gen Tanabe and Kelly Tanabe.*

☐ **Check** out who won. Go to the scholarship's web site. The winning essay or portfolio is usually available. Study it for tips.

☐ **Get extra credit.** Check if you can use scholarship essays or projects as a school assignment or an extra credit project.

☐ **Keep** your counselor informed about your interests. He/she may know of related scholarships.

FRESHMAN YEAR:

☐ **Check** volunteer agencies to see which ones give volunteer scholarships. Consider doing your community service hours there.

☐ **Join** clubs that give scholarships to members. Do this early. Most clubs require at least a one year membership for eligibility.

☐ **Write** your profile to see what scholarship opportunities exist (page 20). List where you and your parents shop, bank, buy gas, and have your utilities. Put them on your list of organizations to contact.

SOPHOMORE YEAR:

☐ **Update** your internet searches.

☐ **Check** with the guidance office for local scholarships that are available and what their requirements are.

☐ **List** local businesses, organizations and clubs. Contact them to see if they offer scholarships or contests.

☐ **Check** with any associations and organizations you, your parents, or extended family members belong to for scholarships and contests.

☐ **Take** the PSAT as practice for the real one which is your junior year. It's the only way to qualify for the National Merit Scholarship.

JUNIOR YEAR:

☐ **Take** the PSAT. The test makes you eligible for the National Merit Scholarships (page 46).

☐ **Talk** to seniors to find out what scholarships they're applying for, especially local ones. Ask them about scholarships offered through their colleges.

☐ **Search** for scholarships weekly, register for online sites, like Fastweb.

☐ **Pick** up local scholarship applications that are available from your guidance office. Get them before the school year ends so you can work on the application and required essay during summer.

☐ **Contact** the athletic department at your selected colleges to apply for sports scholarships (page 82). Do this during the summer. It doesn't matter if you decide NOT to attend a particular college. You can always decline an offer.

SENIOR YEAR:

☐ **Contact** the financial aid counselors at your selected colleges to see what scholarships they have. If you know your major, check with that department to see what scholarships they know are available. Scholarships differ from college to college. This may even be a deciding factor in your final college choice (pages 100 and 137).

☐ **Watch** deadlines! Some are at the very beginning of your senior year. Map out all of your deadlines over the summer so none will be missed.

☐ **Keep** applying. Check to see if any essay you've written can be used for more than one award. Be careful not to get carried away with this—you might waste time and lose money.

☐ **Follow** the directions of the application to the letter. Omitting information can disqualify you.

☐ **Ask** for letters of recommendation early. Allow ample time for your teachers and employers to write and send them. Follow up to make sure they're sent in on time. Also ask for one copy of the letter that doesn't refer to a specific scholarship so that if another scholarship comes up, you may use the same recommendation.

☐ **Notify** the college you've decided to attend of scholarships you'll be receiving.

❝ I ended up with a 'full ride'
—tuition and housing—
just for being a caddy!
Not bad for helping people
chase a little white ball . . .* ❞

Senior, Ohio State U.

*An Evans Scholarship

10

(very cool) things to make your summers count

using your 'free spins'

Summer vacations, long weekends, and winter and spring breaks are 'free spins' in the game of preparing for college. You can sneak in all kinds of stuff—visit campuses, get ahead of required reading, learn new skills, explore careers and majors, earn high school *AND* college credit, make a little money, find a little money, get your community service hours in, prepare for college testing, expand your view of the world—or just contemplate your navel and use the time to discover yourself. Do you have to do *all* of them? NO! Go at your own pace...even if you do one or two things every summer, you're way ahead of the game.

head for the campus

Programs & Camps?
How about . . .
Film making
Fencing
Kayaking
Gold panning
Entomology
Pre-Law
Pre-Med
Rappelling
Blacksmithing
Make-up
Bird watching
Model rockets
Glacier travel
African languages
Drum majoring
White water rafting
Dog sledding
Circus arts
Journalism
Time management
Ice climbing
Adventure racing
Music
Engineering
Golf
did we mention . . .
Football, dance &
web page design?

Almost every college in the U.S. offers fantastic summer programs for high school students. What's your choice? Sports? The arts? Academics? Computer science? They offer great learning experiences and you're able to get a 'feel' for college.

Call local colleges or any others you'd like to 'try on' to see what they offer. Check with your school's guidance office, bulletin boards, and web site for any program they may be hosting or know about. Professional organizations also host campus programs. If there's a field you're interested in, contact the related professional organization to see what they offer and where it's located.

> Exposure is everything for high school athletes.
> If you have a particular college you're interested in,
> go to their summer sports camp.
> The coaching staff notices kids who excel.

Assistant Coach,. Eastern Michigan U.

Most programs are available to sop[...]
over the possibilities *NOW*. Deadli[...]
You'll need an application and a [...]
teacher, counselor, administrator [...]
time to decide which camp to atter[...]
3000 camps, go to:

www.petersons.com/college-search/summer-programs-camps-search.aspx

(Quicklink; Summer Camps and Programs)

Check out these books for even more programs:

Summer Opportunities for Kids & Teenagers
(Petersons)

Kaplan Yale Daily News Guide to Summer Programs
(Yale Daily News)

Summer on Campus
(Shirley Levin)

psssst . . .

Can't afford the programs and camps?
Don't count them out. It's not publicized but financial aid is usually available. If you want to attend, call 'em! Ask for aid. The earlier you apply to ANY program, the better your chances are, especially if aid is involved. Don't wait!

summer camps

Day camps, away camps, supercamps—they're all great places to learn new skills. Look for camps that teach computer or leadership skills, speed reading, time management, sports, art, or anything that interests you. Check with your counselor for camps in your area or for a list of camps, go to:

www.acacamps.org

www.supercamp.com

**ng the summer there are numerous opportunities to
evelop leadership skills**—camps, institutes, confer-ences,
workshops—often on college campuses. For a few, such as
Boys' State and Girls' State, you must be selected by your
principal or counselor, while most are open to all. Check with
your counselor to see what is availble and if you are interested,
let them know.

go to school

Riiiight . . . just what you wanted to do. But it really is
a good time to take one course—in the classroom or
on-line. Take something difficult and you can give it your full
attention . . . or get rid of a Physical Education requirement
and free up an hour during the school year so you can take
another course. If you're a junior or senior, you may want
to take a course at a local college so you can get 'dual credit'
(page 115). A word of caution—check with both your high
school and any college you're considering to confirm which
courses are accepted and for how many credits.

make some bucks

Too young to get a traditional job? Become self-employed.
Get training to become a lifeguard, caddy at the golf course,
detail cars, cut grass, baby sit, walk dogs, paint houses.
In your junior and senior years, get a part-time job or an
internship related to the field you may be interested in
pursuing.

For Boys State go to:

www.legion.org/boysnation

→   →   →   →   →

For Girls State go to:

www.alaforveterans.org/ala-girls-state/

read

During the summer before your sophomore and junior year, get the reading list for the next school year. When you're a senior, read for college. Contact the English departments at the colleges you're considering or check their web sites for required reading lists. Start with books that are common to all the lists. For a general college book list pick up *Reading Lists for College Bound Students* by Doug Estell—or go to YALSA's Booklists for Outstanding Books for the College Bound:

www.ala.org/yalsa/

**www.collegeboard.com/student/plan/
boost-your-skills/23628.html**

66 There was a great summer program
I was dying to go to so I asked the
Rotary Club if they would pay for it
in exchange for me making a presentation to
their group after I returned.
They were, and I did. They were so
impressed, they gave me
scholarship money for college. 99

Freshman, Albion College

visit colleges

Start with walk-throughs just to get the feel of a campus Check out the activities and go to a play or a game. Hang out. And while you're wandering among the students, imagine yourself on campus in a few years. Save the in-depth visits for your junior and senior years. Don't forget virtual tours on the Internet—all colleges have 'em (page 68).

> **66** Going to a math and science
> summer camp sounded geeky,
> but it turned out to be pretty cool.
> We stayed in the dorms so not only did
> I get a 'feel' for college life, I'm 'aceing' math this
> year . . . I used to hate it! **99**

Sophomore, East Kentwood High School

travel

Vacation with your parents and visit a college town. Attend an out-of-state (or at least out-of-your-area) summer program on a college campus or at a camp. Check with your place of worship for any summer missions they may be hosting. Or, do day trips with youth groups. Don't forget to check with the volunteer web sites (page 15) for out-of-state possibilities and see 'Travel' (page 82) for more opportunities.

search for scholarships

Forget the video games for a few minutes and register at a scholarship search site (page 22). Check with your local library to see if they have a scholarship database or if your high school is willing, use theirs. Hit the bookstores and library for scholarship books. During the summer before your senior year, send for scholarship applications, work on your essays, get teacher recommendations, and put necessary portfolios together.

Register with college prep web sites. They're loaded with scholarship info as well as discussion boards, test preps and all kinds of college advice.

www.princetonreview.com

www.kaptest.com

www.collegeispossible .org

www.collegegold.com

www.niche.com

www.fastweb.com/

www.studentaid.ed.gov

http://knowhow2go.acenet.edu/

volunteer

Get your community service hours in now and you'll free up your time during the school year. Feeling ambitious? Start your own do-good group or propose a program to an organization you're working with already. Like what you're doing? Ask if you can come back next year as an intern or if a paid job will be available.

ok ladies . . .

One of the best things that ever happened to female college students is **'Title IX'—the rule that makes colleges set aside money for women's sports.** Want a scholarship? Then use your summers to improve your skills in a sport: golf, tennis, volleyball, field hockey. . .The least you'll get out of it is being healthy.

test prep

Start preparing for the PSAT, SAT, ACT and SAT II tests (page 46 and 85). Find out if your high school or school district offers a summer prep program or look for a summer camp that offers classes. Take the sample tests at the testing organizations' web sites or check out the library and bookstores for prep books.

learn to . . .

66 SPEEDREAD. You either read fast
in college or get left behind. **99**

Freshman, U of Houston.

66 TYPE. PROPERLY. Hunting and pecking just
slows you down too much, especially if you're
trying to take notes in class. **99**

Freshman, U of Wisconsin.

to do's
make your summers count

YEARLY TO-DO'S:

☐ **Call** colleges to find out what types of summer programs they offer.

☐ **Check** with your school's guidance office, bulletin board and web site for summer programs they're hosting or may know about.

☐ **Explore** web sites and books (page 31) for college summer programs. Look for ones related to your interests, ones that teach skills (i.e. computer training), or are just too fun to pass up.

☐ **Call** professional organizations related to your interests for programs they may offer.

☐ **Check** with sport associations (local, national, minor, and professional) for camps and programs. Join or volunteer your services.

☐ **Apply** to programs and camps early. Get in the habit of looking now for programs to attend next year.

☐ **Ask** the program your interested in for financial aid, if you need it.

☐ **Sign up** for a class—on-line or in the classroom.

☐ **Make money.** Save money. Be creative and start your own business or get a summer job.

☐ **Volunteer.** If your high school has a program that gives credit for community service hours, arrange your volunteer hours to get that credit.

☐ **Update** your log. Make note of whatever program or camp you attend, your volunteer work, any summer jobs, extra classes, skills, or travel.

SUMMER BEFORE SOPHOMORE YEAR:

☐ **Get** the reading list for your sophomore year. Polish off at least one book.

☐ **Walk** around a local college campus. Explore campuses nationwide with "virtual tours" (page 68).

☐ **Start** your scholarship search if you haven't already. Sign up at the search sites (page 22).

☐ **Travel.** Ask if your family vacation can include a stop at a college town. If you belong to a youth or church group, check if they're planning any trips—whether it's for the day, a weekend, or longer.

SUMMER BEFORE JR & SR YEAR:

☐ **Look** for summer programs held on the campuses of colleges you're considering. (Remember to express your hopes of attending that college to faculty members.)

☐ **Take** either a high school class or a 'dual credit' class (page 117). Ask your counselor what class is best for you.

☐ **Get** a job related to the major you'd like to study in college.

☐ **Read** at least one book from next year's reading list.

☐ **Begin** your serious visits to the colleges you're considering (page 63).

☐ **Update** your scholarship search with your current GPA and class rank.

☐ **Work** on your scholarship and college application essays during the summer before your senior year (page 107).

☐ **Prepare** for the PSAT (page 46), the SAT, ACT, and SAT II tests.

☐ **Find** opportunities to travel—whether it's volunteering, studying out-of-state or overseas (page 82), or vacationing with your family.

66 I didn't have a clue
what college I wanted to
go to . . . I just took challenging
courses and got good grades
which kept my options open
until I figured it out.
That worked for me . . . 99

Freshman, Tulane U.

> **66** The majority
> of really good students
> aren't walking, talking geniuses . . .
> they just work really hard. **99**

Senior, Salem High School

sophomore
year
keep on keepin' on

The best way to get where you want to go is to set goals . . . whether it's better grades, getting into your dream college, playing a sport, or whatever. Just deciding what's important to you in the long run will help you focus on what you have to do now. Break it down...what is it that you want to accomplish in your sophomore year? The first semester? The first week? What's it take to make that happen? Keep setting goals and revise them as you go. You'll not only get what you want but also gain the confidence of knowing you're capable of just about anything you set your mind to.

to do's
sophomore year

❑ **Sign** up in September for the PSAT (page 45). This one's practice... the real one is Junior year.

❑ **Focus** on your GPA. Take the most challenging classes you can handle.

❑ **Narrow** down your activities to two or three that you'll do throughout high school and may pursue in college.

❑ **Start** a list of colleges to consider. Be sure to go to any college fairs in your area... you'll learn the 'language' of exploring colleges. Use virtual tours and begin thinking about which colleges you'd like to visit in-depth (page 63).

❑ **Take** the personality/interest inventory tests on page 48 if you need help determining colleges or majors. Or, do it just for fun. They ask the questions you need to be asking yourself.

❑ **Plan** your summer. Find programs and camps to attend. Check with your counselor to decide if a summer class is appropriate (page 29).

❑ **Continue** your scholarship search (page 19).

sophomore basics

☐ **Review** for the PSAT, SAT and ACT during the summer (pages 46 and 85).

☐ **Update** your records of activities, volunteer work, programs, classes, and traveling. File information you receive on colleges, scholarships and tests.

☐ **Review** and revise your goals . . . set new ones.

☐ **Think** careers! Talk to people about their jobs (page 51).

. . . homework helper

Stuck? Got an algebra problem that's impossible? Don't understand the symbolism of a book? Science class leaving you dazed? Need the bio of someone famous or want to see and hear a President's speech? Check out the homework help sites before you need them so you know which one works best for you: **www.math.com/**

www.bjpinchbeck.com

www.biography.com

www.khanacademy.org

66 Everyone says that
the key to success in school
is 'getting organized.'
I disagree . . .
It's staying organized! 99

Senior, Salem High School

the tests:
psat & preact

sneak previews

Relaaaax! The tests you can take this year are important but they won't affect your college admission. So, why take them? Two reasons. You'll find out what your academic strengths and weaknesses are (while you can still do something about it) and **because you can.** Any time you get a chance to try something out before it counts—whether it's a test, volunteering to see if you like a major or a career, or taking a program on a campus of a college you're considering attending—*DO IT!*

the PSAT

The SAT's baby brother

Preliminary Scholastic Assessment Test

The 'real' PSAT is given to students in October of their Junior year.

why should you take it in your sophomore year?

- **You can totally blow it** and it doesn't count. It's only practice. But, when taken in the Junior year, thousands of top performing students will qualify to become National Merit finalists which opens the door to thousands of dollars in scholarships and grants.

- **The sooner you take it,** the sooner you'll find out your academic strengths and weaknesses and can link your test results to Khan Academy's online personalized SAT test prep. It's free!

- **Bonus!** Once you take the PSAT you'll begin getting mail (based on your profile and test score) from lots of colleges describing their programs and majors. You'll get an early jump on what's out there.

Don't study, unless . . .

Sophomores do not need to study for the PSAT. But, if you had high scores as a sophomore or you think becoming a National Merit finalist is within the realm of possibility as a junior, study! For everyone else, it's just another chance to practice for the SAT.

the

PreACT
The pre-American College Test (ACT)

**The PreACT is given to sophomores
as practice for the ACT.**

- Your school may offer the PreACT as practice for the junior year ACT. It is not used for scholarships, but does identify your academic strengths and weaknesses so that you and your teachers or counselors can plan your coursework for the rest of high school.

- There are no free ACT prep courses available, but there are a multitude of companies, online and off, that offer tutoring for a fee. The structured feedback from the preACT provides a baseline for those companies to build a program specifically for the student test-taker. And because it's given in the 10th grade, there is plenty of time to set up a program that allows busy students to log in for a half hour to an hour several times a week before the junior year ACT.

The Best Ever ACT/SAT Test Prep

1. Take a rigorous curriculum.
2. Don't study just for a grade, make sure you *UNDERSTAND*.
3. Read for pleasure. It's guaranteed to:
   - increase vocabulary
   - increase speed
   - improve comprehension
   - improve grammar

'psych' yourself out!

online personality tests to find . . .

. . . the right college . . .

www.collegegrazing.com
https://trends.collegeboard.org
www.princetonreview.com/college-major-search
https://www.usnews.com/best-colleges

The US News and World Report site offers a *College Personality Quiz* (see Tools) that identifies the type of colleges where you'd most likely feel comfortable and do well. Links to the colleges, virtual tours and more info are available. *The Princeton Review's Best Fit School Search* helps 10th and 11th graders determine which schools are a "good fit."

. . . the right major . . .

www.mymajors.com
www.myplan.com
http://bigfuture.collegeboard.org/explore-careers

There's an entire battery of career and personality tests that will allow you to zero in on your interests and possible majors. Take one, take 'em all. They're anywhere from cheap to free.

. . . the right career . . .

www.selectsmart.com/collegemajor/
www.careerbuilder.com
https://thepathtocareer.weebly.comskill/?skill-cow.html

to do's
the tests

August/September:

❑ **Tell** your counselor you want to take the PSAT this year—otherwise it may not be offered to you. Find out the date it will be given and how to register. *Note: Stay on top of this one so your counselor doesn't forget.*

❑ **Sign** up. Register and pay for the tests through the guidance office or online at the test websites.

❑ **Check** the test websites for more information and sample questions.

October:

❑ **Go** to the PSAT website and review the test before taking it so that you understand the format.

❑ **Take** the PSAT

December:

❑ **Review** your test scores with your counselor. Get your test book back and go over the questions you answered incorrectly. Talk to him/her about how you can improve in these areas.

❑ **Get familiar** with College Board (SAT), Kahn and ACT websites. They provide personalized study plans for future tests, as well as college/career information and much more.

66 There is no 'magic morning'
when you wake up and
KNOW
what you want to do.
You have to get involved . . .
pay attention to what
interests you . . .
What you're looking for
is a 'FEEL' for what
you really want in life. 99

Junior, Columbia U.

get
a life!

so, waddaya wanna be?

You're only 15 and we're asking you to pick a career?!? Well, no, but we are telling you that you need to get in the habit of talking to people about what they do all day—their jobs! The best way to find out about careers is to talk to the people doing them. How else are you going to find out that your 'dream' job includes a 60 hour work week? Or sleeping in not-so-dreamy motels four months of the year? Or any number of other things you don't want to do? On the other hand, you may get great first-hand information on how to achieve your dream, little known shortcuts, and maybe even wind up with a mentor or an internship.

the only
dumb question...

. . . is the one unasked! Talk to everyone—people you know, people you don't know. The following questions will get you started:

What do you do on a typical day?

What abilities and talents are needed to be successful?

What type of training and education is necessary?

What kind of education and work experiences did you have in order to get this position?

Besides salary and fringe benefits, do you feel rewarded?

Is there a college that you would recommend?

What is the future like for this field? Is there a demand for this position?

If you could do it all over again, would you still want to do what you do?

What kinds of sacrifices and disappointments might I face?

What could I be doing now to prepare for this career?

What professional organizations or journals are there where I could learn more?

Could you give me any advice?

. . . wanna be a rock star?

Read *The Occupational Outlook Handbook...* by the US Department of Labor, it's lots of ink but you'll get the 'nitty gritty' on every job in America—education requirements, salaries, forecasts, and trends. Zero in on the jobs that sound interesting. You can view it on-line or at a library. **https://www.bls.gov/ooh/**

☐ **Talk** with the adults you know. You might hear of a career you never knew existed.

☐ **List** the careers you'd like to have and the names of people who have these jobs. Write a letter, e-mail or call the person you want to interview and set up an appointment. *Don't know anyone? Then:*

- **Call professional organizations** (i.e. Society of Automotive Engineeers). Ask if they could refer you to someone in your area.

    or

- **Flip through magazines** related to that career (i.e. *Psychology Today*). Look for stories that profile people who have the job you want.

    or

- **Call the Human Resources Department** of a business and ask if they could refer you to someone in their company.

    or

- **Talk to people** who work in conjunction with a career. Actors, musicians, writers, and artists have agents and managers who are more accessible than the talent.

☐ **Follow up.** Send a handwritten thank you note after talking with them. Later, reconnect via email to see if they know of any summer programs, jobs, or internships.

❑ **Check** out Career Days. Ask speakers about the college they attended—or wish they had attended.

❑ **Skim** through the books in the career section at your high school or library for jobs that interest you.

❑ **Check** with colleges for major-related summer programs and camps—pre-med, pre-law, computer science, engineering—it's a great way to find out if you like the field AND make great contacts.

❑ **Flip** through a college course catalog for areas of study that seem interesting. Check the prerequisite classes to see if you like them, too.

❑ **Talk** to your counselor if you find a career or field of study that you'd like to pursue. Make sure your classes are on the right track.

. . . career software programs

Some high schools have **career software programs** available to their students. Plug in your interests, abilities, goals, etc. and you're provided with a variety of appropriate careers, their job descriptions, projected income, availability—and which colleges offer related majors. If your high school has this program—

USE IT!

it's

time to start 'the list'

finding the right colleges . . .

. . . to apply to takes some work.
But there's a better reason to start your search
early—**every college has different admission requirements.** That affects how many
AP classes you'll need, if any. You'll know
how important extracurricular activities are—
or aren't. You'll be able to check out course
requirements for specific majors **in addition
to** the college's required coursework. Start
considering colleges now and you'll also have
more time to visit campuses, more time to
compare schools, more time to find out about
financial aid packages, and you'll spend less
time second guessing yourelf. **So start your
list now.**

college
search sites

College search sites match colleges to your interests and abilities. Play at these sites. Change your preferences just a bit and you'll wind up with an entirely different list which might pop up a college that's perfect for you. Sites differ, so try 'em all:

www.collegeboard.org

www.usnews.com/best-colleges

www.petersons.com

www.collegeview.com/collegesearch/index.jsp

www.xap.com

www.collegeconfidential.com

www.bestcolleges.com/careers/

www.salliemae.com/college-planning/

Think about it . . .

There are over 4,000 four year colleges in the U.S. Add to that about another 1900 community colleges—so how do you decide which schools to consider? Start by deciding what's necessary *for you*.

Academics:
What do you want to study? Do you want a specific major or will a liberal arts degree do? Does your area of study require special facilities?

Location:
Where do you want to live? Big city? Small town? Do you want to go to the beach every day or turn into a snow bunny during the winter?

Size:
Do you want to be part of a large student body or a small one? Do you want 100 kids in a class or 30?

Distance:
Do you want to stay at home or be close enough to drop your laundry off for mom to do every two weeks? Or move far away?

66 Deciding which university to attend feels like the most important decision of your life. It's not. Take a deep breath and follow your heart. Every school has as much to offer as you're willing to put into it. **99**

Freshman, Carnegie Mellon U.

You:
Are you more comfortable in a structured class or are you focused enough to do independent study? Do you want to be academically challenged or prefer to skip the brain drain?

Extracurriculars:
What activites do you want to participate in outside of the classroom? Do you want to join a sorority or fraternity?

Sports:
Do you want to play a sport at college? Does the football team have to be Bowl Game-bound every year?

Reputation:
Do you want to go to a 'party' school? Or one that's known for being highly selective?

$$$$$$$:
What's affordable? If you rely on student loans, is a school that costs more still worthwhile?

Lehigh University
27 Memorial Drive, W.
Bethlehem, PA 18015
(610) 758-3100

US News ranking: Nat. U —
No. 53

Website: www1.lehigh.edu

Admissions e-mail:
admissions@lehigh.edu
Private; founded 1865

Setting: Urban

Degrees offered: bachelor's,
master's, doctorate

Calendar: semester

Freshman admission: most selective;
2017-2018: 13,871 applied, 3,489
accepted. Either SAT or ACT required.
SAT 25/75 percentile: 1270-1430. High
school rank: 63% in top tenth, 89% in
top quarter, 99% in top half.

Early decision deadline: 11/15
notification date: 12/15 Application
deadline (fall): 1/1 Common application: yes TOEFL requirement: yes
Under-graduate student body: 5013,
full time 62% part-time; 55% male,
45% female; 0% American Indian, 8%
Asian, 4 % black, 9% Hispanic, 3%
multiracial, 0% Pacific Islander, 64%
white, 9% international; 27% from in
state; 65% live on campus; 38% of students in fraternities, 45% in sororities

Most popular majors: 13% Finance,
10% Mechanical Engineering, 6%
Accounting, 5% Marketing/Marketing
Management, 4% Chemical Engineering.

Expenses: 2018/2019: $52,930,
room/board $13,600.

Class size: 39% have fewer
than 20 students; 47% have between 20 and 50 students;
14% have 50 or more students.

Financial Aid: (610) 758-3181. 42% of
undergrads determined to have financial need; average package $46,861.

from: US News & World Report, 2018/2019
Edition America's Best Colleges

must reads

Each year *Newsweek* and *US News and World Report* publish special college editions. School profiles and requirements, along with updates, great advice, tips, sample tests, college rankings, and contact information are included:

US News and World Report: America's Best Colleges

Newsweek: How To Get Into College

66 If you want to know what a college is looking for in a student, call the admissions department ... We always like to talk to a customer. 99

Admissions Counselor, Mt. Saint Clare College

pricey schools?
don't count 'em out

Your Expected Family Contribution (EFC)—the amount of tuition your family is expected to pay (page 94)—stays roughly the same no matter how expensive a school is. Schools want a diverse student population and to get that, they may be willing to help you. If you total your federal aid, scholarships and work-study programs, your student loan may be the same as a less expensive school.

very 'selective' schools?
consider counting them out

Sure, 'Ivies' are prestigious, but a study sponsored by the National Bureau of Economic Research showed that middle-class students earned a higher income later on when they attended *a college whose average SAT scores were 1000* as opposed to *a college whose average SAT scores were 1200.* Taking two students who are equal, the student who attends a slightly less selective institution will probably have higher grades, a higher class rank, stand out more to faculty, and have more confidence in his or her abilities.

grades, SATs . . . fuh-ged-about-it!
Want to go to a college that doesn't give grades? How about one that doesn't care about your SAT score? Want to study computer gaming? Design your own degree program? Or go to a school that has a golf course on campus? Read Donald Asher's *Cool Colleges for the Hyper-Intelligent, Self-Directed, Late Blooming, and Just Plain Different.* A great way to find colleges you'd never think of on your own.

gurus, coaches & advisors
on-line

The sites below will offer you answers quickly and from a lot of different sources: college advisors, coaches, admissions folks, high school and college students. Check out the bulletin boards, Q & A pages and chat sites.

www.mycollegeguide.org/guru

www.collegeconfidential.com

www.nextstepu.com

http://knowhow2go.acenet.edu

(Be sure to sign up for the newsletter!)

'Best of the Best'

www.allaboutcollege.com

This site lists colleges in every state in the U.S. with links to their web sites, PLUS links to each college's chat room so you can see what students on campus are talking about, PLUS e-mail addresses to each admissions office—a quick way to request information.

'the list'

☐ **List** what you want in a college (page 56).

☐ **Register** at the college search sites (page 56) to help develop a list of colleges to research. Vary your location, class size, etc. to produce more choices.

☐ **Read** the college editions of *US News and World Report* and *Newsweek* (page 58). Pick up the new edition yearly.

☐ **Add** any schools that may be recommended by family, friends, counselors, teachers, magazines, or books to your list.

Next . . .

☐ **Visit** the college web sites and take a virtual tour of the campuses.

☐ **Register** at the colleges' web sites and request an information pack (you can also call the admissions office for this).

☐ **Call** the admissions office if you have any questions about the requirements.

☐ **Plan** on-campus visits to narrow down your choices further (page 63).

66 Don't rely on the
mood swings of friends . . .
I was considering Notre Dame
until I talked with a buddy
who was a first semester
freshman there . . . He had
NOTHING good to say about the
place! Based on that, *I didn't even
apply.* He now raves about
how great the school is . . . Guess
he got over his 'freshman funk'.
My advice?
Take a formal tour. 99

Sophomore, Indiana U.

the campus visits

the test drive

You'll want to start visiting colleges the summer before your junior year. Tours with student guides take about an hour or two; but most colleges have programs that allow you to stay overnight in a dorm, sit in on classes, meet with teachers and coaches, and interview with admissions officers. Call the admissions department to schedule your visit and find out what extended information sessions they offer. You should also check to see if they have a specific day set aside where all high school students are invited to explore the campus. If it's mid-week, you'll need to clear it with your high school.

TRIP TIPS

**Freshman,
Virginia Tech**

"I have a lot of unhappy friends because they had an 'image' of their college and it turned out completely different. Tours can provide a 'reality check.'"

Senior, Hope College

"We drove 3 hours just to 'look around' — never realizing that if we had called ahead, we would've been given a tour of the campus, the dorms, met a professor in my major . . . I walked away from a $24,000 scholarship because I was 'unimpressed' when I hadn't really given the school a chance."

Sophomore, William and Mary

"College is a whole lifestyle and you're not going to experience it on a tour. Plan on spending one or two nights with a student at (the) college."

**Sophomore
U. of Colorado**

"Lose your parents. Walk around campus by yourself. They're not coming to school with you."

Sophomroe,
Penn State U.

"I'd never even seen the campus! I just figured that millions of kids had come before me and made it ... As long as you don't expect perfect ..."

Freshmen, Converse College
"Visit the school. Visit the town. Visit the stores. Visit the people."

Sophomore,
Georgetown U.
"Trust your gut. If you don't feel right, it's not the school for you."

Mom,
U. of Arizona
"Give it the night-time test. If it's Tuesday night and there's a lot of partying and loud music coming out of the dorm rooms .. is that you? Are you going to be able to study?"

Junior, Miami U. Ohio
"DO NOT SET FOOT ON A CAMPUS IN AUGUST! My parents wanted to squeeze in a college visit before my senior year so our entire family flew out for a tour. The people there were really nice—both of them! The place was a ghost town! It weirded me out ..."

65

best times for
campus visits

Mid-week. Mid-week visits allow you to get a feel for day-to-day life right down to eating in the cafeteria and sitting in on a class. You can meet with professors and/or admissions people. Be sure to call ahead.

Weekends. You'll get a good taste of the social scene... and seeing how many kids spend weekend nights studying will give you a clue as to the academic scene. If most students leave on weekends, it's a 'suitcase college.'

Summer. BUT only when classes are in session and the faculty you want to see will be there. Probably a little more laid back than usual . . . check to see if the dorms are air-conditioned.

Holidays. Your holidays (Good Friday, Presidents Day, Spring Break) may not be theirs in which case a visit could be perfect. Forget Christmas. Everyone's gone in December the minute exams are over.

Exam Week. Check the college exam schedule. It may be all right for a day visit with admissions but certainly not an overnight.

you may want to ask...

Have questions ready for admissions officers and students. Ask the same ones on all visits so you can compare fairly. These can get you started:

For admissions officers:

What percentage of freshmen return for sophomore year?

What makes the major you're interested in special at this school?

What kind of scholarships are offered? Availability? Who's eligible?

Does the school provide tutors? Is there a fee or is it free? Is there a mentoring program?

Is dorm living available for all four years? How much off-campus housing is available?

Do most students join fraternities and sororities? How do students who don't join socialize?

What do the tuition costs include? What other expenses can I expect?

Are campus jobs available? Are there businesses to provide part-time jobs and internships for students?

What are the safety issues on campus? What safety measures are in place?

What are the important campus issues?

For students:

What's the best thing about this college? The worst?

Do the professors teach or TAs? How accessible are the professors?

How big are classes? What's your favorite class?

Do students stay or go home on weekends?

How close are restaurants? Shopping?

What transportation is available? Can I have a car? Parking on campus?

Where's the shopping district? Restaurants?

What's fun to do? Where are the movies? Concerts? Sporting events?

the admissions
interview . . .

Very few schools actually require a personal interview . . . however, **it can be to your advantage to request one.** It allows admissions to put a face with the name on the application and gives you a chance to provide more information than just what's on the application. When it's down to the wire as to who gets in and who doesn't, chances are you'll have an advantage over someone who didn't interview. Here are a few pointers to make your interview successful:

- **Review the college catalog and website** before your visit. Don't ask questions that are answered in either.

- **Make a list of questions** you'd like to ask and also make a list of things you'd like them to know about you.

- **Keep your parents out** of the interview.

- **Send a thank you *note*** . . . not an email.

. . . look for links

Look for links to students' web pages when you're visiting a college website. They provide more 'up close and personal' info as well as email addresses of students so that you can get the 'inside line' directly from the students themselves.

visit
if you can't . . .

Don't scratch a college off your list because you can't visit it. There are lots of ways to determine whether it's a good fit for you . . .

- **USE the college's website.** You'll find student life info, links to majors, research opportunities, where students are getting jobs, and more.

- **Get on the mailing list.** Sign up on the website and you'll receive all kinds of information.

- **Check out the financial aid pages** on the website. Use the school's **net price calculator** to calculate your tuition, and all other expenses.

- **Virtual tours.** You can actually "see" a college without getting off your sofa. Almost every college website has a virtual campus tour and there is a variety of websites that provide virtual tours. Here's a couple:

    www.campustours.com
    www.ecampustours.com

- **Facebook & Instagram**. Find out what actual students think about their school. Type in the college name, add "Class of 20XX" and you'll see posts and pictures. Just ask a question—students are always happy to offer their opinions.

- **Compare** schools using the most up-to-date, comprehensive and reliable information available:

    https://collegescorecard.ed.gov/

campus visits

Before:

☐ **Call first!** ~~Contact the admissions office or go online to see what the options are for visiting the campus. Ask:~~

- ~~How far in advance does your visit need to be scheduled?~~
- ~~In addition to tours, are there other activities?~~
- ~~Is there a scheduled 'Open House' for all high school students?~~
- Can you spend a night in a dorm?
- Can you meet with a professor? A financial aid adviser?
- Can you meet with a coach? (The NCAA allows 'unofficial visits'. . . for a look at the rules and an Unofficial Visit Form, see below.)

https://www.tamiu.edu/athleticcompliance/documents/
Unofficial%20Visit%20Form.pdf

☐ **Make it official.** Want to 'drop by' a campus and just wander around without an official tour? Don't. You won't learn nearly as much. Besides, a record of your visit shows admissions that you are genuinely interested in their school.

☐ **Do some homework.** Look through the college's website to see what majors there are, what courses you might like, what special living and learning programs they have...you'll learn just enough to have lots of questions for the tour guide . . .

☐ **Make a list** of questions that you can ask at every college visit. (page 67) It makes comparing colleges an 'apples to apples' thing.

During:

☐ **Ask for a map** of the campus so you'll be able to refer to it later. Note where the freshman dorms are in relation to classrooms? Where is your intended major located? Where are the social and recreation areas? Parking? (Is there a fee?)

☐ **Check out** the classrooms and labs (i.e. music rooms, studios, theater, etc). Visit the library. Are the facilities up-to-date and will they accommodate what you want to study?

☐ **Check out** the dorm rooms, bathrooms, common rooms. Can you choose the type of accommodations you want—single, double, suite, apartment? Roommate?

☐ **Eat in the cafeteria** or have a latte' in the café. Eavesdrop on conversations. Notice student behavior, dress, diversity. Do you fit in?

☐ **Get the email address** or phone number of whomever you meet with in case you have more questions later.

☐ **Grab a student newspaper** or two. Read bulletin boards for activities, clubs, opportunities, and campus and local issues.

☐ **Check out** what deals the university offers for computer hardware and software.

After:

☐ **Keep score!** A campus visit scorecard allows you to do just that. Print off multiple copies at the site below and fill them out after each visit.

https://www.gearup.wa.gov/file/college-board-campus-visit-scorecard

66 "It's a good thing that I didn't see my dorm room before I enrolled here, or I might have gone to another school ... This has been an awesome experience—great friends, great classes...I hate to think I could've missed all that ..." 99

Sophomore, Notre Dame

11

junior year
on your mark,
get set . . .

The time is now to make sure you're on the right track for the colleges you want to apply to. Intensify your scholarship search, study for SATs/ACTs attend college fairs, do in-depth college visits, find out about financial aid... and most important of all FOCUS ON YOUR GRADES! College admission folks rely heavily on your junior year GPA! They want to see grades rising—not falling. Beyond that, every extra thing you can do this year is going to make your life a lot easier as a senior.

Whenever I could, I avoided teachers who were tough graders—especially if they required a lot of papers.
It was good for my GPA but the downside is I had a really hard time my first year of college . . . especially in my freshman writing course. 99

Sophomore, Spelman College

to do's
junior year

Through The Year . . .

☐ **Concentrate** on your GPA. Keep your grades high and your courses as challenging as possible.

☐ **Get real.** At this point, you know your GPA and class rank and have your scores on the PSAT and maybe the ACT or SAT. That allows you to narrow your college list using 'real' numbers to decide which schools are a fit. Compare your numbers to various colleges:

collegescorecard.ed.gov

☐ **Get** on the mailing list of colleges you're considering. Contact the Admissions office or go to the colleges' websites to do that.

☐ **Continue** your college visits through the year (pages 63-72).

☐ **Attend** career days, college fairs (page 79) and financial aid workshops.

Fall:

☐ **Meet** with your counselor. Be sure your classes are on the right track for the colleges you're considering and that you're meeting graduation requirements.

☐ **Register and take** the standardized tests. An ambitious schedule would be to take the PSAT (page 46) in October, the SAT in November and the ACT in September or December. Then you'll know which test format is better for you and where to focus your efforts for a retest, if needed.

❑ **Talk** to your coach if you want to play for a college
team or apply for an athletic scholarship. (page 84)

❑ **Contact** the US military academies NOW if you
want to apply. Find out about the individual schools
and their summer programs at:

www.defense.gov

Winter:

❑ **Review** your test results with your counselor to
decide which test(s)—ACT, SAT, SAT II's to take
in the spring. Register for the test(s).

❑ **Set up a plan** to study for whichever test or tests
you've decided on. You can link your PSAT or SAT
results to Khan Academy's online personalized test
prep (it's free) or consider the online ACT test prep.
(page 85-92)

❑ **Combine** your scholarship search with a job.
Many companies will help pay for college if you are
working there part time in high school. McDonalds,
Starbucks, Taco Bell…just to name a few.

Spring:

❑ **Sign up** to take the AP exams for the AP courses
you've completed.

❑ **Before** school closes for the summer, get an unofficial transcript with the classes you've taken, your
GPA, class rank and quartile so that you can begin
completing college applications during the summer.

❑ **Consider** taking a summer class. You can start earning college credit by taking 'dual credit courses' or classes at a community college. (page 117)

❑ **See** your counselor for an NCAA Clearing House form if you want to play sports in college (page 84).

Summer:

❑ **Compile** writing samples, put together portfolios, and work on audition tapes if the colleges or scholarships you're applying to require them.

❑ **Know** when college applications drop. Some are available as early as July 1. The Common App drops on August 1. Get started . . . especially if you're applying Early Decision or Early Action.

❑ **Work** on your essays for the applications and for scholarships. The topics may be available before the application is. (page 107) Check.

❑ **Zero in** on what teachers you want to ask for recommendations (page 124). Work on a resume to provide them (page 103).

❝ I got most of my college applications and essays out of the way in the summer . . . there's too much going on when school ramps up in the fall. ❞

Senior, DeWitt High School

let's play . . .

Ask the right questions and you may win admission to the college of your choice!

Am I on the right track to complete my graduation requirements? Will I have enough math, science, and language classes for college?

Can I get a pass/fail grade option for electives so it doesn't affect my GPA?

What scholarships do you know about? What scholarships have been awarded to students? Does the school have a scholarship search program?

Are there any finacial aid workshops or seminars for my parents?

Should I take advanced placement classes, dual credit courses (page 115), correspondence, on-line courses, or any summer classes?

What are dates for the SAT and ACT this year? Does the school offer prep classes or materials?

Will the school be hosting a college fair or college night? Will a large college fair be held locally? Do local or state colleges hold weekend infor-mation worshops?

Are there any contests, panels, or any other opportunities to represent my school?

(If you`re interested in the military) How can the military help me? Whom should I contact for more information?

66 I hadn't even heard of this college,
let alone it's aviation program.
I talked with their rep at College Night . . .
and here I am. 99

Freshman, Northwestern College

come to the college fair!

College fairs give you a chance to talk with representatives from colleges you're considering and expose you to schools you never knew existed.

▷ Your high school may offer one or there may be one offered at another school in you district or in a district nearby. Check with your guidance office and watch the newspapers. Call to see if you are allowed to attend.

▷ To find out if the college you're interested in will be at any fair, go to the college's web site or call the admissions office.

super-sized!
the NACAC fairs

The National Association for College Admissions Counseling host huge fairs with hundreds of colleges in attendance. You may have to drive to another city, even another state, but attendance is well worth it. For dates and locations go to:

www.nacacnet.org

college week live!

Visit hundreds of colleges and have questions answered by admissions experts via live chat *without leaving home!* View college planning presentations by college reps from top schools across the US.

www.collegeweeklive.com

why knock yourself out?
the AP dilemma

 AP coursework prepares students better for the rigors of a college classroom.

 Selective schools EXPECT that you will have taken them.

 GPA rules! That's particularly true for less selective schools as well as for many scholarships. AP's aren't a factor... an 'A' is an 'A'.

 AP courses are smaller, cheaper, and most students say 'a whole lot easier' than the equivalent college course. Load up.

 You'll end up taking upper level classes as a college freshman—before you've gotten used to the pace of college coursework.

 Does admissions look more favorably at a 'B' in an AP class than an 'A' in a regular class? Ask 50 admissions officers and get 50 different answers! Your best bet... take the AP class and work your tail off to get an 'A'.

66 AP's are serious business...
they're for serious students . . .
I've had students take them
just to be in a class with a friend
or just to be able to say they were taking it—
the results were disastrous. 99

High School Counselor

For more info: www.collegeboard.com

> ❝ It's worth taking as many APs
> as you feel you can do well in.
> In college I was able to fill my schedule with
> interesting electives instead of boring basics. ❞

Junior, Rice U.

> ❝ I took two AP English classes and THEN found
> out the college only allowed credit for one...
> **Check out which college accepts which
> AP credits before you take them
> because they're a lot of work!** ❞

Freshman, U. of Chicago

**https://apstudent.collegeboard.org/creditand place-
ment/search-credit-policies**

money well spent . . .

"...you pay $100 to take an AP exam . . . but if you receive a qualifying grade on that exam you'll earn college credits, **which can be worth anywhere from $300 at a state university to $3,000 at a private school.**"

Sue Collins in *Newsweek's How to Get Into College*

The International Baccalaureate (IB) Program... offers a choice of the Diploma Program (two years—junior and senior—of intense study) or opt for IB certification in specific subject areas. Relatively few American high schools offer IBs but their popularity is increasing. Watch out: many students say IBs are more difficult than college classes. But they all say IBs prepare you for college-level work. For more information and the schools that offer the IB Program, go to:

www.ibo.org

see the world...

There are organizations that can help wit information, opportunities, arrangements, student IDs, and discount fares. Whether you want to take time off before you start college to study abroad during high school or college, or be involved in a volunteer or work exchange program these sites can help. Not the globetrotting sort? Do it in North America. Some of the opportunities:

great stuff!

IIEPassport.org

THE search engine for high school and college students searches by language, country, or study. This site has quick notification on programs that fit you and ones that may be of interest, an on-line student guide for FAQs and more.

www.nationalservice.gov/programs/americorps

Stay on home turf. Volunteer as a mentor, build houses, clean parks and streams, or respond to disasters in a 10 month full-time residential program for 17 years and older. Get a great experience AND dollars to pay for college or student loans (and perhaps a living allowance).

www.unitedplanet.org

Volunteer in Russia, China, Peru... explore a biosphererereserve or go on a culinary tour. Do a high school semester or spend summer living with a host family and study overseas. Language schools and study abroad programs are available for HS and college students.

www.vfp.org (Volunteers For Peace)

For a 2 - 3 week program, international volunteers perform community service in overseas workcamps. Students from at least 4 countries make up each group. Cultural and social sharing and discussion are encouraged. Work camps for ages under 18 are limited to France and Germany.

www.experiencegia.com

GLA offers high school students ages 14-18 the opportunity to volunteer around the world. Care for orphans at the base of Mt. Kilimanjaro, build homes in the Caribbean, protect endangered species in the Galapagos, or teach sports and build a school for kids in Peru. It's cultural immersion, adventure and community service certification all in one. A family program is offered as well.

www.isecard.com

Get your International Student Identity Card and save on travel, rooms, museums, events and entertainment. Specializing in student travel, the network of 500 organizations covers 100 countries. Also the site offers overseas work exchange programs.

You can study abroad while in college, too. The 'study abroad' office at your college will be able to find a program that suits your major.

www.studyabroad.com

HS'ers can spend summer on European college campuses (scholarships available!). Or find out what's available before and during college.

www.unv.org

The United Nations volunteer program offers opportunities overseas, on home soil or on-line. Also links to organizations specializing in short-term and long-terms volunteer service, medical service, wildlife conservation, humanitarian efforts, disaster relief, and more.

www.statravel.com

CT excels in travel possibilities for students and will even help you design your own around-the-world trip. Apply for a student discount card (ISIC), or book student fares for air or rail. Language courses, work/internships, and study abroad programs are also offered.

www.cityyear.org

The youth service corps asks for volunteers, ages 17 and older for a full year of community service, leadership development and civic engagement. Programs are in major US cities.

the
jock clock

So you want to play a sport in college . . .?
The time is *now* to start the process. The NCAA (National Collegiate Athletic Association) has very strict guidelines and timelines concerning recruiting and student to coach/college contact. So to start off, tap your coach's wisdom and enlist his support. And while **the biggest myth around is that a high school student is not allowed to make contact with a college coach—you can, and *you should*.**   There are all kinds of things you may not be aware of—such as completing the **NCAA Clearinghouse** form by the end of your junior year and before July 1 if there's even the slightest chance you'll play a college sport. Ask for it in the guidance office. To sort the myths from the facts, go to:

www.eligibilitycenter.org

https://www.fastweb.com/student-life/articles/

seven-myths-about-college-sports

❝ It was a win-win.
I loved playing ball and
—scholarship or not—
there were colleges
interested in me that
wouldn't have been otherwise . . . **❞**

Graduate, U. of Michigan

don't panic

Even if you're the world's worst test-taker there's hope for you. Along with being able to take the SAT and ACT numerous times to improve your score, you can take practice tests to ease your anxiety. There's help everywhere. An industry has been built around helping you get a better test score. And in case your test score doesn't reflect your stellar GPA, relax. Admission departments know that some students don't test well and take that into consideration. In fact, a few colleges don't even consider the tests at all . . .

THE 'BIG BOYS' . . .

(SAT)
www.collegeboard.com

(ACT)
www.actstudent.org

Which test do I take?

"Neither the SAT nor the ACT is 'easier' or 'harder' than the other—but different types of students usually do better on one than on the other."

Anthony James-Green, ACT/SAT Tutor

 All colleges accept either test.

 The decision may be made for you if your state requires one test in particular. Then, the decision is whether to take both tests in order to determine which you score better on, so that you can focus your efforts on that one when prepping for a retest. For more info:

https://blog.collegevine.com/which-is-easier-the-sat-or-the-act/

https://blog.prepscholar.com/is-the-act-easier-than-the-sat

https://greentestprep.com/resources/sat-prep/act-vs-sat/

(This site provides a step-by-step process to figure out which test is better for YOU!)

 Not much difference? If you've taken both tests and there isn't a significant difference in the scores, then stick with the test that your high school requires since you're likely to have better resources for preparing for it.

When should I take it?

Best-case scenario #2: You've been able to take your chosen test at least twice and have the scores you want by the end of your junior year.*

Accomplishing that somewhat ambitious goal, means that you would possibly take the PSAT in October of your junior year (page 46), then take the ACT later in October and the SAT in early December. The scores on those tests will help you decide which test to focus on for a retest in the spring of your Junior year. With that, your summer and senior year are free to work on applying to colleges!

▷ **7 times a year**—that's how many times both the SAT and ACT are given. Look up the dates online and set up your test calendar. Avoid dates when you are busy with activities or sports, if possible, and allow enough time to prepare for the tests.

▷ **For a better score,** get Geometry and Algebra II under your belt before taking the tests.

▷ **Applying Early Decision?** Check with the college for the last safe test date. The October test in your senior year may be too late.

▷ **The early bird gets the worm.** Merit scholarships are first-come, first serve and often have October or early November deadlines. Your application and test scores may have to be submitted together. Call admissions and ask.

▷ **Allow time for one test** in your senior year just in case you need it—preferably October, but December at the latest. Ask admissions.

▷ **The last time** you'll be able to test and still get the results to your college on time is November/December of your senior year — ask admissions what is the last test score they will accept.

*Best-case scenario #1: You get the score you need the first time you take the test.

▶ **Forget the PSAT** in your junior year if you took it as a sophomore and your score was nowhere near what it takes to be a National Merit finalist—unless you want more practice for the SAT. But, if you had a high score, do some serious prepping for the Junior year test. It could mean a National Merit Scholarship.

▶ **Interested in the Military Academies'** summer camps? You will need to have taken your ACT or SAT in the fall of 11th grade as the applications are due in January.

Should I retest?

▶ **Yes, if** a higher score would improve your chances of being admitted to the school of your choice or if there's a scholarship or merit award that you would be eligible for. Chances are that greater familiarity with the test and having completed more coursework will improve your score, If it doesn't, most colleges allow Score Choice so you can send only the scores you want them to see. Btw, you need to put in a lot of test-prep time to improve your scores.

▶ **No, if** you've already met the threshold for admissions or a scholarship. But, confirm those numbers with the admissions office.

> 66 My ACT score was 26 and good enough to get me into the college I wanted to go to ... so I wasn't going to re-take the test. My mom called admissions and found out I was one point short of the score I needed for a merit scholarship. I re-tested and got the point ... and $24,000 over 4 years!" 99

Freshman, Central Michigan University

test day tips

Test 'stand-by' if you missed registration. Call the testing organization to see if you can take the place of a 'no-show'.

"**Take a practice test—on paper.** The real test is on paper. It's the only way to get a real 'feel' for the test."
Freshman, Ohio State U.

"**Read the instructions on the sample tests** until you've got 'em down 'cold'. You can pick up a couple of minutes during the real test."
Sophomore, U. of Michigan

Want your school to see only your best score and not the dogs? Both the ACT and SAT allow you to do that. Forfeit the free score reporting at the time of the test. Then notify ACT ($12) and SAT (free) which scores to send after you've seen the results.

Know where you made your mistakes! **Get a copy of your SAT test from College Board** ($18). It'll help you focus your studying for the retest.

"**I took an energy bar** with me and ate it between sections . . .at least it kept my stomach from growling."
Freshman, U. of Michigan

"I knew where the school was (test location) but I didn't know the street was torn up. I wasn't late but I didn't have time to relax, either. Do a 'test drive' before test day."
Sophomore, U. of Wisconsin

Make sure your **name appears the same way on all your tests and college applications.** The test companies and colleges will have a harder time matching tests to applications if you don't.

what's it take?*

As you can see by this sampling of SAT and ACT scores from schools around the US, 'selectivity' is not based solely on test scores. (ACT: 2 digits, SAT: 3-4 digits)

Perfect scores: SAT—1600, ACT—36

most selective

Harvard 1460-1490
MIT 1420-1570
Notre Dame 1410-1550
Duke 1480-1590 (SAT) and 32-35 (ACT)
University of Michigan 29-33 (ACT)
Oberlin 1310-1490 (SAT) and 29-32 (ACT)
US Airforce Academy 29-32 (ACT)

more selective

Purdue 1160-1390
George Washington University 1280-1450
Auburn University 24-30 (ACT)
Antioch College 27 (ACT)
University of Texas 1240-1450
Tulane University 29-32 (ACT)

selective

University of Arizona 1050-1290
DePaul University 22-28 (ACT)
Illinois State University 21-26 (ACT)
University of Colorado 24-30 (ACT)
Howard University 1090-1300

less selective

Albany State University 22-26 (ACT)
Bethany College 17-22 (ACT)
Fisk University 17-23 (ACT)
Morgan State University 16-20 (ACT)
Marian College 980-1210

least selective

Alabama State University 15-23 (ACT)
University of Bridgeport 920-1090
Northeastern Illinois 16-20 (ACT)
Southern Vermont College 15-19 (ACT)

US News & World Report, 2018 - 2019

to do's
'the tests'

☐ **Create** a calendar for taking the PSAT, SAT, ACT and any other tests. Find the dates the tests are being offered on their respective websites.

☐ **Take** SAT Subject Tests as soon after you've taken the course as possible—if they are required.

☐ **Decide** whether to include the essay on your test. Know that it is scored separately and does not impact your score. It adds 40 (ACT) or 50 (SAT) minutes to the testing period. Some colleges require it, so find out if any colleges you are applying to do.

☐ **Register** at least six weeks prior to the test date. If you want to be assured that you will test at your first choice location, register much earlier—especially if your school is a test site.

☐ **Know** whether the colleges you're interested in allow you to Score Choice—submit only the test scores you want. (A few colleges want to see them all.)

☐ **Test** 'standby' if you missed the registration deadline.

☐ **Ask** your counselor for a fee waiver if you can't afford the test. Also ask for disability accommodations if you need them.

Test day:

Do:

- Make sure you know the location of the test. Allow plenty of time to get there if you haven't been there before.
- Layer your clothing. Some test centers are hot, some are cold.

Bring:

- Your admission ticket
- Photo ID
- Your high school code
- The code numbers of colleges you want the scores sent to
- Pencils - #2 soft lead with good eraser – no mechanical pencils (essays are written in pencil only)
- Approved calculator. Extra batteries.
- A wrist watch that has no alarm or sound
- Water and a snack (only allowed at break)

Don't bring:

- Any electronic device, other than permitted calculator (this includes your mobile phone, smart watch, fitness band, headphones, camera)
- Highlight pens, colored pens or pencils
- Books, notes, scratch paper

❝ A kid was kicked out of the test for having his cell phone with him. He forgot to turn off the ringer. I wouldn't risk it! **❞**

College Confidential

aid
money 101

get it right—now!

It's important to get familiar with the financial aid process now not only because it's so darn complicated but because the fiscal year on which your financial aid package is based begins in January of your *SOPHOMORE* year and ends December 31st of your *JUNIOR* year. If your family needs to plan its finances, they need to do it before the base year begins. And don't ignore FAFSA guidelines because you think your family is ineligible for financial aid. You'll lose out on the opportunity to at least take advantage of government loan programs. **The truth is . . . virtually every college student in the U.S. qualifies for some type of financial aid.**

the language of
financial aid

FAFSA: Free Application for Federal Student Aid. You must fill this form out even if you do not expect to receive aid from a college. **You can't get a federally-backed student loan without this form.**

CSS/Profile: College Scholarship Service Profile, a non-government FAFSA. Not all colleges require this form. Check with the schools you want to apply to for the proper forms (some colleges even require their own financial application).

EFC: Expected Family Contribution. The amount your family is expected to pay based on their specific circumstances and finances.

SAR: Student Aid Report. You will be sent this form after completing the FAFSA. Colleges use this form to determine your aid package.

Need-based: College grants and scholarships that are issued based on your financial need.

Merit-based: College grants and scholarships that are issued based on your academic, athletic or artistic talent. Ethnicity is also sometimes considered.

Grants: Money from the government or college that **does not** have to be repaid.

Loan: Money from the government or private lender that **does** have to be repaid.

Scholarships: Do not have to be repaid. Can be **institutional** (from the college) or **private** (outside source).

Work study: Need-based program of subsidized jobs through the college. Students usually work up to 20 hours per week.

Subsidized: Interest on a loan **does not** accrue while student is in school

Non-subsidized: Interest on the loan **does** accrue while student is in school.

PELL Grants: Federal money for low-income students that **does not** have to be repaid.

Perkins Loan: A federally-backed need-based loan direct from a participating college. Interest does not accrue while student is in school.

Stafford Loan: Government sponsored loans to students. Subsidized Stafford Loans are need-based; non-subsidized are not. Either can be obtained from banks, savings and loans, or other lenders.

PLUS Loans: Government sponsored loans to parents come at a higher interest rate than Stafford loans.

State grants: Money from a state that is given to resident students who are attending in-state schools. Programs differ from state to state.

just the facts,
ma'am

Financial aid packages vary from college to college and depend on family circumstances, a student's abilities and talents, and how each Financial Aid Officer (FAO) interprets a student's needs. **One thing is certain: the more you understand financial aid, the more likely you are to receive it.**

Some basics that cover *EVERYONE*:

- **Almost every family qualifies** for some type of aid even if it's only a federally backed loan at lower interest rate.

- **The amount your family is expected to pay (EFC)** stays roughly the same at expensive schools as at cheaper schools. It's the aid package that is adjustable.

- **Financial forms do not reflect** family circumstances that may limit your ability to pay (i.e. medical expenses). You can talk to the Financial Aid Officer (FAO) directly and have your EFC adjusted.

- **Don't put family assets in a** student's name. Student's money is always assessed at a higher rate.

- **You can negotiate** financial aid packages from colleges (page 140).

- **You'll pay more** at out-of-state public schools. Base tuition is usually doubled at least.

- **Aid packages offered** to the student for the freshman year may change for the next three years.

A student's income

---

is assessed at a

---

higher rate than parents'.

After exemptions, parents are expected

to contribute about 5% of their income.

Students are assessed at 35%.

---

money moves

It's your parent's income that takes center stage when your eligibility for financial aid is being considered. Some families elect to 'lower' their income by controlling when one-time or unusual income (such as a bonus or money from a real estate transaction) is made. Because college financial aid packages use a base calendar year that begins January 1 of your 10th grade year and ends December 31 of your junior year you need to understand the ins and outs of financial aid or consult your financial advisor now. **Any 'money moves' need to be done before or after that base period.**

A great website to help parents prepare financially for college is:

www.savingforcollege.com

In order to get the maximum...

In order to get the maximum money available

to you, take out a Perkins or Stafford Loan

before applying for a PLUS Loan.

everything you ever needed

the sites

Use these web sites to find out about the financial aid process, scholarships, grants, loans, work study programs, use a financial calculator, and download forms and instructions. Visit as many as you can—they're loaded with tips, strategies and advice.

www.finaid.org

www.fastweb.com

https://www.ed.gov/

https://www.collegeboard.org/

www.xap.com

www.collegepossible.org

www.petersons.com

www.collegeview.com/collegesearch/index.jsp

https://www.salliemae.com/college-planning/

httpr://studentedge.org/

www.collegegold.com

state aid

All states provide need and merit based aid. The good news is they're usually more generous than the federal government. Even if the feds turn you down, your state may do something for you. But state aid is usually given to residents who plan to attend school in-state and residency requirements are strict. If you're thinking about attending another state's public university, **check with your state to see if it has a reciprocal agreement with other states.** That would allow you to transfer your aid. For links to your state's aid office, go to:

www.students.gov

to know about financial aid . . .
. . . and where to find it

hard copy

Books that address specific financial aid situations line the shelves at bookstores and libraries. For a good general overview of the financial aid process with plenty of advice, tips, strategies, guidelines, worksheets, forms and directories, try:

How to Pay Wholesale for College 2018-2019
(Andy Lockwood)

Paying for College Without Going Broke 2018 Edition
(Kalman Chany)

The Ultimate Scholarship Book 2019
(Gen and Kelly Tanabe)

Never Pay Retail for College
(Beth Walker)

The Financial Aid Handbook Revised Edition
(Carol Stack and Ruth Vedvik)

'the' magazine

Want to know what any college costs? Tuition? Room and board? How many students receive financial aid? How much financial aid do they receive? Pick up a copy of *US News & World Report: America's Best Colleges.* Here's a sample of what you'll get:

PRINCETON:
Expenses: 2018/2019: $49,055 tuition, room and board: $18,520. **Financial Aid:** 60% qualify for aid. The average aid package $53,100.00.

Important to know!

the financial campus visit
dicker & deal

The financial aid package should be part of the college selection so do a financial campus visit—even if it's only by phone. It's only fair that the FAO answer questions such as:

▷ **Will my financial need affect** my admission chances?

▷ **How will applying 'Early Decision'** affect my financial aid package?

▷ **Does the college use** its own financial form? What are the college's deadlines?

▷ **What costs are not included** in the aid package? Room and board? Books?

▷ **Is there an academic requirement** for aid renewal? Any other conditions?

▷ **How will my aid package differ** from year to year? Will it decrease?

▷ **What merit and need-based aid is available** and what is the criteria?

▷ **What is the average loan debt** for a student at the time of graduation?

▷ **Does the college assign work-study** jobs? What kind of jobs are available? How many hours per week?

▷ **Does the college include PLUS Loans** in the financial aid package (page 140)?

▷ **If the financial aid package is insufficient,** under what conditions will the FAO reconsider?

money 101

Junior Fall:

☐ **Get** your parents involved in the financial aid process so they can make any decisions that will impact your financial aid before the 'base calendar year' ends December 31st of your junior year.

☐ **Take** the PSAT in October which may qualify you for the National Merit Scholarship. If not, you'll get practice for the SAT and connected to colleges by major and GPA via College Board's free student search service.

☐ **Schedule** your first ACT and SAT before Christmas if possible so you can see if your scores auto qualify you for scholarships at certain colleges. If not, you'll have time to retest.

☐ **Contact** the financial aid office at the colleges you're interested in or chat online. Ask what GPA and test scores qualify for scholarships and merit awards.

☐ **Watch** for 'college night' or financial aid programs or seminars offered by your high school.

Junior Winter:

☐ **Find** out what kind of financial aid is offered by your state (page 96).

☐ **Get** the US Government's publications *Student Guide*, *Funding Your Education*, and *Looking for Student Aid*, downloadable at:

https://www.usa.gov/financial-aid

or call **1-800-4FED-AID**.

☐ **Prep** for the (ACT/SAT) test! Even a one point increase on your score can mean thousands of dollars in tuition money! (page 88)

☐ **Open** accounts with all the scholarship search sites. Set up automatic notifications when new scholarships are posted.

☐ **Make** a spreadsheet listing scholarship due dates and contact information. Aim for 3 new scholarship opportunities every week.

Junior Spring

☐ **Attend** financial aid programs or seminars offered by your high school (with your parents).

☐ **Organize** your upcoming college visits. Contact admissions or go online to sign up. Ask to meet with a financial aid counselor.

☐ **Find** a summer job, the experience looks good on a resume' and you'll make some money.

Junior Summer

☐ **Make** a list of the financial records you will need to have completed for college and scholarship applications. (Fafsa, tax returns, CSS Profile...)

☐ **Do** a financial aid campus visit (on-site or by telephone) during the summer the financial aid office isn't busy (page 100).

. . . a big summer!

This is a big summer The more you do now, the less stress you'll have your senior year. (see page 77)

how
to build your 'resume'

bragging rights

There's a bonus to putting a resume together now. If you have any weak spots, you'll be able to see where they are while there's still time to do something about them. A resume is a place to show off your hard work. **It can speak volumes for you, especially when you're not there to do it yourself.** Use your resume to apply for jobs and internships, attach one to scholarship applications, and give one to those whom you've asked to write a letter of recommendation. Last but not least—save some for those college applications!

66 There's only an itty-bitty space to 'tell something significant about yourself' on most college applications. Resumes are a great way to 'sneak' in a little more. It's good marketing. 99

High School Counselor

putting
'you' on paper

Create a resume that highlights your strengths and interests via your activities in and out of school. Use active verbs to describe your involvement, i.e., organized, assisted, completed, created, led, participated, etc. but don't exagerate the facts. No one expects grandiose achievements from a kid in high school—they're looking for solid character.

Give a copy of it to your college guidance counselor for his review, and also in case he is contacted by a college admissions person who wants additional info about you. Also, provide copies to any teachers who are writing letters of recomendation. Sample resumes and formats can be found at:

https://www.collegeboard.org/

https://www.groovejob.com/resources/resumes/
sample-resume.html

https://www.thebalancecareers.com/part-time-job-
resume-example-for-a-teen-2063248

https://www.livecareer.com/career/advice/resume/
resume-tips-for-teenagers

to do's
resumes

Include:

❑ Personal information

- Name
- Address
- Phone number
- E-mail address

❑ Scholastic information

- Name of high school
- Class rank, GPA
- SAT, ACT and SATII scores

❑ Academic achievements

- Honor roll
- Advanced placement classes
- College credit classes
- Internet classes
- Awards, nominations, recognitions, citations or special projects in subject areas
- Tutoring or mentoring roles

❑ Computer Skills

- Programs you know
- Skills (web site design, programming)

❑ Workshops, camps, programs, seminars, projects, special classes, and competitions

❑ Work experience, internships

❑ **Club involvement**
- School
- Community
- Church

❑ **Special interests** hobbies, pursuits

❑ **Volunteer work** on-going and one time events

❑ **Athletic** participation and achievements

❑ **Leadership roles**
- Holding office in class, sports, clubs
- Taking initiative or responsibility for projects
- Leadership camp participation

❝ Don't cheat yourself by leaving out
accomplishments that are not formalized
. . . If you've been a caregiver to a sick
parent or you've invented a
computer game
—include it in your resume. ❞

High School Counselor

the essay

seal the deal

While one essay won't guarantee your getting into a college, a good one helps—and a bad one can 'tank' your application. And you won't be writing just one essay. You'll need at least one for each college application, not to mention scholarships. Save a part of the summer before your senior year to brainstorm ideas and work on rough drafts so you have plenty of time for rewrites and polishing. Don't forget the basic ingredient of a good essay: YOU! Essays are your chance to add dimension to those numbers and checked boxes on your application. Bring a little life to that package!

essay
do's . . . .

DO answer the question.
Questions are often open-ended to allow you room
for expression. But make sure your essay fits.

DO get personal.
This essay's about you! Be passionate.
If it sounds like 300 other people
could have written it, you're missing something.

DO write a good lead.
Hook 'em with the first sentence
and they'll want to read the rest.

DO read
other essays to see what works.

DO check your essay
to see how you come across. Likeable?
Friendly? Interesting?

DO give your essay a rest.
Write it and then put it down for a
couple of days or weeks if you can.
Fresh eyes can tell you what's missing.

DO ask for help —
from your English teacher or an editing service.

DO edit and rewrite.
Even Hemmingway did.

. . . . and don'ts

DON'T try to be funny. . .
unless you really are and can carry it off like a pro.

DON'T suck up!
They know you want to go to their college.
Why else would you be doing all of this?

DON'T go over the word count.
Officials have to read thousands of essays. Too long
and you may be disqualified on a technicality.

DON'T use big words when little ones will do.
If you use them incorrectly, it'll count against you.
Plus you run the risk of looking arrogant.

DON'T let your parents
write your essay. You don't want to sound
like you're 45 years old.

DON'T plagerize or buy an essay.
This is about YOU. Besides there are
plagerizing programs that officials use and
they'll spot you in a minute.

DON'T use your friends or
relatives to critique your essay. They're too biased.
Use an English teacher or an editing service.

DON'T be negative!
Don't whine, complain or ask for sympathy.
Don't ever try to explain
a bad GPA or ACT/SAT score.

" . . . one student lost a $5,000 scholarship because he submitted an essay that was written for a different college.
He was admitted but lost a great scholarship because he was lazy and took a shortcut. **"**

Admissions Counselor, U. of Washington

insightful sites

For detailed how-to information, tips, and samples, you can't beat the internet. The sites below offer a variety of resources and while someof their services are fee-based, they also provide a lot of information for free:

www.myessay.com/
(Numero uno! Excellent information on every aspect of writing an essay!)

https://studymoose.com/essay-topics
(lots of good suggestions for essay topics)

www.essayedge.com/
(editing services, competitively priced)

www.teenink.com/CollegeEssays/index.php
(sample essays submitted independently)

www.thoughtco.com/college-admissions-4132565
(Articles and links to good tips and sample essays.)

www.scholarships.com/financial-aid/
college-scholarships/scholarships-by-type/essay-
scholarships/
(focuses on essays for scholarship applications)

the essay

☐ **Review** last year's essay topics on-line at your colleges' web sites.

☐ **Find** out if your scholarship applications require essays.

☐ **Check** out the bookstores and libraries for books on writing college essays.

☐ **Brainstorm** a list of topics that you could use.

☐ **Narrow** down your topic selection by writing brief outlines and eliminate weak ideas.

☐ **Write** a draft of your essay(s). Don't read it for a few days, then . . .

☐ **Edit** and rewrite your essay(s). Make sure it answers the question asked.

☐ **Tailor**, blend in, or change your essay in some way to be more appropriate and fit the question asked if you're submitting it to more than one college.

☐ **Proofread**—don't spell check—your essay. Computer spellcheckers can't tell the difference between 'know' and 'no'.

☐ **Ask** two objective people (i.e. English teacher/counselor) to review your essay.

☐ **Make** sure your final copy is neat and clean.

66 The first 3 years
of high school is what
gets you INTO college . . .
your senior year
is what KEEPS you there. 99

Admissions Officer, U. of Michigan

12

senior year
. . . GO!

If you've had your act together along the way, senior year is the 'payoff'— good times, good friends, getting into the college of your choice, and looking ahead to the future. While you may be tempted to 'ease up' on academics—don't. Senior year is your launch pad. . .the more challenging your classes, the easier your adjustment in a college classroom. This is not the end of your journey, it's the beginning and you'll want to make sure that you're well prepared for what lies ahead.

Fall:

☐ **Create** a master calendar of deadlines. Include college applications, test registrations and test dates, scholarship applications, housing, and financial deadlines.

☐ **Last chance** to take the SAT or ACT. Register and be sure to request the scores be sent to your colleges.

☐ **Finalize** your college list and download the admission applications if you didn't do it in the summer. Start working on them.

☐ **Ask** for letters of recommendation from teachers, employers, and coaches if your applications require them. (page 124)

☐ **Discuss** your college plans and financial aid preparations (page 139) with your counselor.

☐ **Make sure** your high school transcripts and records are correct and up-to-date.

☐ **Attend** college fairs and financial aid workshops.

☐ **Start** working on the FAFSA with your parents. You can submit it beginning on October 1st. It is the main determinant of how much you're expected to pay and how much financial help you will get. (page 137-138)

☐ **Take** the SAT Subject Tests if needed.

☐ **Apply** 'Early Decision' or 'Early Action' Confirm the college's deadline. (page 125)

☐ **Complete** your applications, proofread and send! The sooner the better for schools with 'rolling admissions.' (page 121)

☐ **Make sure** your high school has sent your transcript, essays, recommendations and test scores. Many colleges provide you with a code or ID to access your application status. Use it to make sure all the necessary documents have been received.

Winter:

☐ **Schedule** visits to colleges on your final list.

☐ **Continue** to research and apply for scholarships, particularly at the schools you've applied to.

☐ **Ask** your counselor to send your mid-year grades to your colleges. Follow up to make sure they did.

Spring:

☐ **Compare** financial aid packages you've been offered. Contact the schools' financial aid offices for any questions.

☐ **Prepare** for the AP or CLEP tests if you're taking them. A good score will earn college credit.

❑ **Decide** on a college and notify the admissions office by May 1st. Notify other colleges who have accepted you that you will not be attending.

❑ **Send** in your enrollment and housing deposits by the deadline. Some colleges have a shortage of on-campus housing and it's first come, first serve.

Summer:

❑ **Notify** your college of any scholarships you have received.

❑ **Start looking** for a 'work-study' job for the fall if that is offered in your aid package. Some schools have a directory of work-study jobs online. Your school's career center or faculty from your major also might be able to help you. Or, you may want to ask for a deferral until later in the year.

❑ **Start** your reading assignments for freshman year once you get your course schedule. Check with the department for titles. Or there may be a 'freshman common reading.'

❑ **Kick back** and enjoy the summer with high school friends or travel with your family.

66 Dual credit is basically a college scholarship! Is it harder? Yes. But you're only sitting through the course once and saving thousands of dollars. Plus, you still have your high school support system. 99

High School Counselor

getting a
head start...

Earn college credit NOW! Want to get basic college classes out of the way? Save tuition? Groove into college-level work?

▷ **Dual Credit classes** let you earn high school and college credit. These classes are offered on a college or community college campus, sometimes at a high school, and even on the internet at college websites.

▷ **Early College High School** programs provide an opportunity for students to earn a high school diploma at the same time they are earning an associates degree or 2 years of college credit towards a bachelors degree. It is a very unique high school experience and essentially affords students two years of college—tuition-free!

www.earlycolleges.org

▷ **Community College classes** are a great way to get core college classes out of the way since credits are usually transferable. Consider taking one or two classes during your senior year and/or one during the summer before college.

▷ **Distance learning** is done by taking college courses online (page 132).

beware. . .

Some colleges may refuse to accept some or all credits or will want you to take an AP exam to prove you've learned the material. Talk with admissions at the colleges you're considering to see what are the best classes to take before investing time, effort and money.

66 Kids apply to schools
they don't even want to go to
just to say they 'got in.'
It's like 'get a grip . . .' 99

Freshman, Michigan State U.

the
art of applying

deadlines, details, decisions

Don't trip up on a technicality.
Every college has its own deadline and usually
there's more than one. In-state students may have
different deadlines than out-of-state students.
Then there are separate deadlines for housing
and financial aid. Each college has its own
application forms. Even colleges that use a
'common application' will have an additional
form for you to complete. Miss a deadline or fill
out an application incorrectly and—no matter how perfect you are for that school—you
may disqualify yourself from being accepted.
Pay attention to deadlines and details so you
can deal with the most important 'D': deciding
which college you'll attend.

applications...
where and how many?

Application fees range from $25 to $60.
You'll want to apply to more than one, but applying to more than six colleges may be wasting money that could be used for books. Apply to academically appropriate schools with various levels of selectivity:

▷ **'Reach'** schools are the most selective schools on your list; probably your first and second choices. Your chances of getting in are about 20%.

▷ Schools whose numbers (SAT/ACT scores, GPA and class rank) match your numbers should be your second group. **Your chances of getting in are about 50/50.**

▷ Include at least one **'safety'** school—a college that fits your needs. Because of your credentials and their selectivity, you'd be a prize candidate—*one they'd offer scholarships or additional financial aid.*

❝ Look at what the WHOLE school
has to offer—not just what
you want to major in.
You may want to
change your major.
And remember,
you'll be spending
at least 4 years of your life there. ❞

Freshman, Texas Christian U.

admissions...
rolling and deadline

Apply to six colleges and it's likely you'll find six different application policies. Read applications carefully and follow directions to the letter. **Omitted or incorrect information will cause your application to be returned.** Pay attention to the type of admissions each school uses:

> **Deadline admissions:** Applications are sent in by a deadline and only then does the school begin it's admission process.

> **Rolling admissions:** Applications are accepted or rejected as they arrive. Most large state schools use this process. The schools get choosier as they get closer to the deadline date. **Applying early is vital.**

> **Special filing dates:** Out-of-state students may have different deadlines than in-state students.

applying
on-line

Save LOTS of time and apply to several colleges at once by using the 'common application' website. It tracks all due dates and what forms are missing. Super easy!

www.commonapp.org

(Also check to see if your state has a common app for in-state schools!)

https://commonblackcollegeapp.com/

(Apply to over 30 historically black colleges for one fee.)

Link to hundreds of colleges' online applications and/ or downloadable forms via:

www.collegenet.com/

admission tricks

If you don't need financial aid—let 'em know. If the school is short on funds or loaded with applicants who need aid, it may help.

The 'hot' college that everyone in your class wants to go to will be harder to get accepted. Too many applicants from one school can cut down your chances. If there's a school you want to go to, keep your mouth shut!

Wanna let the colleges know you're really interested? Ask for an interview with the admissions officer and talk to the professors in your desired major. You'll stand out as an applicant.

Colleges give points for geographical diversity (state and rural/urban), being related to an alumni, and ethnicity. Consider schools in various locations and don't forget schools family members attended.

A college is more likely to accept you if your major is in an 'under-enrolled' area. Ask the admissions officer how your choice of major might affect your chances.

Stand out! Colleges give extra points for talent and athletic ability. Let 'em know what you can do.

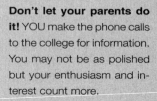

Don't let your parents do it! YOU make the phone calls to the college for information. You may not be as polished but your enthusiasm and interest count more.

Don't just apply to 'reach' schools. Include at least one 'safety' school in the bunch. You don't want to end up with 6 rejections and no place to go.

Market yourself! If you do something special—art, photography, music, etc.— send a sample of your work.

Feel like the 'real' you can't be presented in a common application? **Submit added information or explanations.** Make sure your social security number and name is on every page.

Call every school you've applied to and **make sure your application has been received and is complete.** If anything is missing, get it to them pronto!

Send thank you notes after interviews, visits or if an admissions officer has been extremely helpful. You'll get your name in front of them again.

Didn't make the 'cut' at the college of your choice? Find out what community college that school uses as its 'feeder' school. Do your 2 year core curriculum there and you'll be able to transfer. It's a great way to save money, too.

Apply Early Decision only to your first choice school — applying ED is like adding 100 points to your SAT score.

If you know alumni from the college—a relative, employer, volunteer supervisor —ask them to write a letter of recommendation for you.

how to get
good recommendations

Select teachers who know you well (if you have a choice). It's a nice touch to include a letter from a teacher related to your proposed field of study.

▷ **Give each teacher a copy** of your resume and a personal statement of your goals. Include the colleges you're applying to and why you chose them.

▷ **Remind the teacher** who you are. Include any writings from his/her class or remind him/her of any special projects.

▷ **Include any necessary forms** as well as a stamped, self-addressed envelope. Include the deadline date!

▷ **Ask early. . .** before everyone else does. At the end of junior year, they'll have the summer to write it. Do a polite follow up to make sure the letter was completed and sent.

▷ **Follow instructions.** If a school requests a letter from a language teacher, don't substitute. If they want two letters, don't send three.

▷ **Send thank you notes**—handwritten, no emails!

> 66 Don't TELL me you 'need' a
> recommendation . . .
> I'm honored to be ASKED. 99

High School Counselor

early decision

Early Decision is an option offered by some schools. Simply, you apply early and you find out early if you're accepted. Early Decision can lessen your senior year load but it has pitfalls:

▶ **It's binding.** If they accept you, you've got to go to that school. If you apply Early Decsion make sure it's your first choice school.

▶ **You can't compare financial aid** packages. Because you're committed, the school may not feel the need to be generous to you. They'll use the money to entice another student.

▶ **Early Action** works the same way as early decision but it's non-binding. Check to see if your school of choice offers Early Action as well as Early Decision. Weigh your options carefully.

▶ **Don't slack off** on regular applications to other schools.

don't even think about . . .

applying **Early Decision** to more than one school. Many schools share applicatin lists. If your name appears on more than one list, you can be dropped from all of them.

making the
final decision . . .

"A&M had my friends but
SWT had the majors I was interested
in. It was hard, but I left my friends.
It's been a good choice . . .
I couldn't be happier."
**Sophomore,
Texas State U..**

I always thought I wanted a small school...
but my mom made me apply to a large
university too. That's where I ended up...
I love the environment, the diversity,
and all the experiences that go with it.
College is more than books.

Freshman, U. of Texas

"Don't choose a
college to be close to your
boyfriend. I fell out of love with
him AND the college.
**Freshman,
Converse College**

Look at the freshman support
services, especially if you're an athlete. You're
not going to have the time other kids have to
figure out all the new student 'issues.'

Sophomore, U. of Texas

Everyone thinks it's good to go away. But I missed home. I missed the place that I had hated living in my entire life. I came back. It's been a great experience . . . college IS what you make it.

Sophomore, U. of Nevada, Reno

"Both of my sisters went here. I just followed them. I'll always wonder how happy I could have been someplace else."
Freshman, Texas A&M

Take it from a 'transfer,' I learned the hard way . . . look for an environment with things to do outside of school.

Junior, U. of Minnesota

"Listen to your heart. Pick a college that fits YOU."
Sophomore, U. of Minnesota

This school's in a tiny little town in the middle of nowhere and it's been the most fabulous four years I could imagine. On campus and off, everyone feels like 'family.'

Freshman, Murray State U.

"I didn't 'make' a decision. I just went where my friends went. It was SO big. I felt SO lost. Great school—not for me. Marion is a tenth of the size but it's so 'me'."
Junior, Marion College

127

have you been
waitlisted?

Being put on the waiting list offers you a ray of hope but **be realistic.** Schools can wait list anywhere from 100 to over 2,000 students, many times with little chance of getting in. If you really want to be accepted, don't just sit there:

> **Let 'em know you want in.** Call the admissions department and tell them they're your first choice. Ask what you can do to increase your chances.

> **Send extra letters** of recommendation, especially ones that pertain to your field of study or highlight how your being on campus would benefit the college.

> **Being 'em up to date.** Get your grades up and tell them. Let them know about any new honors or awards you've received or new involvement in community service and activities.

> **Ask for another interview** and razzle dazzle them.

> **Let them know** if you don't need financial help. Many times coffers are nearly empty and paying your own way could make a difference.

> **Consider the schools** that accepted you. *You're their FIRST choice.*

. . . can't get in fall semester?

Ask about **'midyear admissions'**. In other words, enrolling in spring, winter, or summer? Many colleges are beginning to offer this option to keep seats full.

66 ... more students should consider
small liberal arts colleges ...
where endowments are spent on
the pupils themselves,
not supporting 22 Division 1 sports. 99

Seppy Basili, Institute for Academic Excellence,
in *Newsweek's How to Get into College 1999*

vacancies...

The National Association of College Admission counselors' (NACAC) web site posts colleges that have openings for their freshman class AFTER the May 1 deadline. Hop onto the site and click onto the 'Space Availability'. Survey for state-by-state listings of colleges you can still apply to: **www.nacacnet.org**

deferred admissions

Many colleges allow students who have been accepted to take up to a year off before starting classes. Deferred admissions are granted to allow you to work full time, clarify your career goals, travel or volunteer. You won't be allowed to take classes for credit during that time but, depending on your travel or volunteer work, you may be awarded credit hours. Each school's policy is different, so check with your admissions officer **before** you apply.

66 If there's something that would tell us
more about you, include it with your application.
It does make a difference—especially if you're
borderline for admission. 99

Admissions Officer, Michigan State U.

options...
the 'CC' edge

Community Colleges have definite advantages. They provide a lot of flexibility in terms of time, money, and the type of degree you can obtain—two year associate degrees, certification, or simply taking core classes closer to home.

▷ **Yearly tuition at a CC is less** than $2,000, half the cost of a 4 year public college, and only a tenth of the cost of a 4 year private college. Do your core curriculum at a CC and you'll save up to 50% on your bachelor's degree. Plus, you're still eligible for scholarships and federal grants and loans.

▷ **SATs and ACTs are not considered.** You will need a high school diploma, its equivalency and/or pass a high school 'exit' exam.

▷ **Classes are offered at various times** during the day, evenings, and weekends, and many have online courses—a plus if you want or need to work.

❝ Get rid of a course you're dreading by taking it at a community college during the summer before classes start. I wish I had ... my math course sucked up so much time during the first semester that I got crummy grades in everything. ❞

Junior, Southern Illinois U.
(Been There Should've Done That—995 tips for making the most of college)

> ❝ Your first day of class
> is the first day of your career.
> You better be prepared to 'own' this...
> otherwise you'll drown. ❞

Admissions Couselor, Full Sail

the fast track
Career Schools

Do you have a passion? If you know exactly what you want to do with the rest of your life and you're in a hurry, there may be a school out there just for you. BUT, **forget football games, fraternities, and cutting class**—these 'no-nonsense' programs are intense, accelerated and *professional.*

▶ **Every course you take** will be related to the field or industry that you intend as your career. If you're in Video Production, your math will include such things as figuring the wattage necessary to light a movie set. If you're in Video Game Programming, your English may include developing a promotional package for a new game or writing a review. Sociology will consist of analyzing how technology effects the world.

▶ **It can be fast**—12 months to 4 years, depending on the type of degree or certification necessary to complete the program.

▶ **You are 'plugged in'** to your field—to the latest trends and technology—as well as job contacts.

for accredited . . .

career schools go to:

www.accsc.org

career schools

the short list...

3-D Animation	Film
Architectural Drafting	Golf
Art	Graphic Design
Aviation	Hospitality Management
Broadcasting	Interior Design
Business	Legal Administration
Computer Aided Drafting	Nursing
Computer Information Systems	Personal Trainer
	Photography
Culinary Arts	Recording Arts
Dental Hygiene	Show Production
Digital Media	Turf Management
Fashion Design	Video Game Design

For more information, apptitude tests, a discussion of your options and links to school:

www.computer-schools.us

www.petersons.com

www.publichealthdegrees.org/

www.technical-schools.us

university of internet...

You can get a degree on-line—or just take a few classes. But it takes a lot of discipline! Finding an online school isn't difficult but make sure the school is accredited. You can find degree & program offerings, rankings, 'Diploma Mill Police' and more at:

www.geteducated.com

http://oedb.org

www.worldwidelearn.com

**Application deadlines will vary from
school to school. Keep your eye on
due dates—they're typically Oct 1,
Dec 1, Jan 1 or April 1.**

Fall:

☐ **Narrow down** your college choices and create a spreadsheet for the information on each college to include deadlines, cost, scholarships, GPA, ACT, SAT averages, majors available.

☐ **Know the process!** College application procedures vary from high school to high school. Know what your responsibility is in the process. Most schools have senior information meetings for students and for parents. Go.

☐ **Be** sure your final SAT/ACT scores have been sent to your selected colleges.

☐ **Decide** if you want to apply Early Decision or Early Action. Remember, these deadlines will be earlier.

☐ **Ask** your teachers, counselors and/or coaches for recommendations (page 124).

☐ **Download** your college applications at the colleges' websites or check the application help sites (page 121). They begin dropping as early as July 1 which means you can get a head start. Get applications for housing and financial aid at the same time.

❑ **Complete** college applications and essays.

❑ **Make** copies of all digital applications—for colleges and scholarships. Save to your desktop or a folder.

❑ **Verify** your high school transcript. Order official transcripts to be sent directly to each college on your list.

❑ **Make copies** of each completed application for your files.

❑ **Submit** your applications online, BEFORE the deadline—in case of any 'glitches'.

❑ **Check** your email for a confirmation that your application has been received and whether there are any missing items such as test scores, recommendations, financial aid info…. If so, get it to them immediately. If you don't receive an email within a week, call admissions.

❑ **Call** the admissions offices of your colleges at least once to verify your application is complete and nothing is missing. If anything is missing, get it to them immediately.

Winter:

❑ **Withdraw** your other college applications immediately if you are accepted Early Decision.

❑ **Begin** the financial aid process (page 137).

Spring:

☐ **Check** housing deadlines, deposits and refund procedures. Make deposits where necessary to put a hold on dorm space. If you haven't decided which college to attend yet, only send in those deposits that are refundable.

☐ **Review** and compare acceptance and financial aid award letters (page 140).

☐ **Choose** your college and notify the schools you won't be attending. You must do this to free up space for another student.

☐ **Call** the admissions officer if you are waitlisted. Ask how you can improve your application or better your chances.

☐ **Send** in your enrollment deposit.

☐ **Verify** your housing situation with your college. Apply for housing deposit refunds from the colleges you won't be attending.

☐ **Make** your reservation for orientation and registration.

☐ **Give** a copy of your acceptance letter to your counselor for your file.

☐ **Send** thank you notes to everyone who has helped you. Inform them what school you'll be attending. Don't forget to include the staff in the guidance office!

'Senioritis' is NOT your new Spanish teacher

66 I just felt like I didn't need
any more hard work!
The worst part was that it continued
into my first semester at college
. . . not a good thing. 99

Sophomore, Cornell U.

66 If you're thinking about dropping
academic classes listed
on your application, think again.
Colleges DO review your senior records. 99

High School Counselor

Senioritis: (n., se'-ne-or-i-tis; from the Latin meaning "time to party") A condition that affects 12th graders who believe they can coast through the last year of high school. Symptoms include falling GPAs, lower class rank, missed opportunities to lessen freshman college load. Rare cases have resulted in grades so low, accepting colleges have reversed their decision. **Prescribed cure:** continued reality checks and acting in one's own best interest.

money 102

. . . getting it.

Financial aid is a 'first come, first served' operation. Wait too long to send in your forms and the coffers will be empty. So, get your applications in as soon as the process will allow. **For FAFSA, that means beginning October 1** of your senior year. FAFSA relies on numbers from your parents' most recent 1040 income tax form which has already been completed and filed, so easy deal. If your college requires a CSS/PROFILE (only 400 colleges do), it must be filed at least four weeks before your college's 'priority filing date'.

the forms . . . .
fafsa

(for basic information on FAFSA and the financial aid process, see Money 101, page 93)

FAFSA is the federal form for student aid. It is used to determine how much money your family will be expected to pay and how much financial aid you are entitled to. Enlist your parent's help and apply for FAFSA online at:

studentaid.ed.gov/sa/fafsa

Even if you think you won't be eligible for need-based aid, fill out the FAFSA. You won't be able to get federally-backed loans (which come at a much lower rate) or some scholarships without filing it.

the fsa id...

To complete the FAFSA you will need to register online for the FSA (Federal Student Aid) ID 1-3 days before you want to work on the form. Don't give your FSA ID to anyone or allow anyone to create an FSA ID for you—it's a legal signature. Get your FSA ID at: **fsaid.fed.gov**

need help . . . ?

- **Watch for a workshop** at your high school or call the counseling office to see if there's one scheduled.

- **Download a free worksheet** ahead of time so you can gather all the required financial and tax documents.

- **Call 800-433-3243** if you want to talk to a live person, or hit the 'Live Help' button when filling out your application.

- **College Goal Sunday** is sponsored by the YMCA and offers personal FAFSA counseling on weekend events across the country.

css/profile

Almost 400 schools and scholarships require the CSS Profile in addition to FAFSA. The CSS profile application is located on the College Board website, as is the list of universities that require it. The form is available as of October 1, it takes about an hour to complete, and the cost is $25.00 for the first school and $16.00 for each additional school. Fee waivers are available. Fill out the CSS Profile 2 weeks prior to your University application date. The financial report is sent directly to each university from College Board upon payment. Visit College Board for a complete list of instructions and a link. **www.collegeboard.com**

special applications...

Some colleges, especially the more selective ones, have their own financial form in addition to the FAFSA or Profile. Call the college's financial aid department to find out what forms are needed, the deadlines, and to request any special application.

don't **NOT** do it!

Thinking of NOT filling out the FAFSA form? You'll hurt yourself in more ways than one:

- Some scholarships and grants will disqualify you if you haven't sent in FAFSA.
- Many student employment situations won't consider you unless you apply for aid—even if you believe you won't qualify.

comparing aid packages...

Two financial aid offers of $13,000—are they equal?
Not if one is mostly grants and the other mostly loans.
Before you accept—or reject— any offers, use the
'Compare Aid Award' tools at:

www.collegeboard.com

yes, you can appeal a financial aid package

Didn't get enough aid from your first choice school? Did
another school offer a better aid package? Before you write
off a school or remortgage the house, ask the financial aid
officer to reconsider the aid package.

▶ **Explain that the school is your first choice** but
another school has made a better offer (if that's
the case).

▶ **If there are extenuating family circumstances**
(medical bills, divorce, loss of a job), explain them.

▶ **Don't lie.** The FAO will want supporting evidence
for any claim you make, including a copy of the
other school's aid package.

**bigfuture.collegeboard.org/pay-for-college/
tools-calculators**
(Calculate your EFC, cost of college, loan repayment,
value of college, etc)

. . . when student aid, isn't

PLUS Loans should never be included in a
school's financial aid offer. PLUS Loans—
federally backed loans to parents—are
designed to help parents deal with their
EFC and any unmet need.

> " Check out your state schools,
> especially for financial help.
> Nevada high school grads
> get a $10,000 scholarship to go to
> Nevada state colleges. That helps! "

Freshman, U. of Nevada

'FinAid' tips

Don't wait to get an acceptance letter to apply for aid. By that time, most of the aid will be gone.

College financial aid deadlines are different—and usually earlier—than federal and state deadlines. Miss a college deadline and you may only qualify for loans.

Early Decision could mean early deadlines. Check with the financial aid officer for deadline dates.

Even if you don't qualify for federal aid, you may qualify for state aid. States are more generous than the federal government.

Watch those scholarship deadlines and requirements. **Missing one or having an incomplete application will jeopardize your eligibility— even if it's not your fault.**

Empty spaces on your financial aid forms will count as errors and cause delays. Enter '0' in lines that don't apply.

Call the financial aid offices to confirm your application has been received and is complete. If something is missing, get it to them quickly.

Correct errors immediately. Errors slow down the process which can ultimately limit your aid.

Keep copies of EVERYTHING! You'll need them if your forms get lost or to correct errors.

Ask your parents to call the Human Resources Department where they work and **ask if the company will pay any of the tuition for employee's children.**

> " Borrow only what you need. . .
> I always took the 'max' since there were
> a lot of things I needed—
> a $1,000 bike, flat screen TV, sound system—
> I'll be paying for them for the next 20 years! "

Senior, San Francisco City College

loan-ly choices

Nearly two-thirds of all college graduates now have student loans that they are paying back. The sage advice from all of them would be to "borrow as little as you possibly can."

The best and least expensive loans are from the Federal government (Stafford, Perkins, Plus, etc) Unfortunately, one out of five private loan borrowers don't take advantage of the federal loans they are eligible for, according to Marc Scheer in *No Sucker Left Behind.*

It pays to understand the loan process:

www.finaid.org/calculators/loan payments.phtml

(Students can estimate what kinds of salaries they will need to earn in order to pay back various loan amounts.)

www.finaid.org/loans/

(Colleges that offer low-income students financial aid packages without loans—also known as *free tuition!*)

www.efc.org   **www.ticas.org**
www.salliemae.com   **www.bankrate.com**

www.simpletuition.com

https://collegeparents.org/

R.O.T.C.
atten-shun!

▷ **The ROTC provides scholarships** at about 600 schools nationwide. In exchange for active duty or part-time duty in the National Guard or Reserves after you graduate, you'll get the vast majority of your tuition paid PLUS a graduated living stipend of anywhere from $250 to $500 a month.

▷ **Enlist in any of the service branches** after you graduate and Uncle Sam will help pay off that student loan.

▷ **If your parents are or were in the service**, loan assistance is also available.

For information on all the ways the military can help you, go to:

www.affordablecollegesonline.org/rotc-guide/

one more fafsa tip...

All males must register with Selective Service by their 18th birthday. Not registering will disqualify you from receiving federal aid. You can register on the FAFSA form or, go to:

www.sss.gov

FYI . . .

FAF$A

- The earlier you send in your FAFSA, the more money is available and the more you're likely to benefit. You can start filing on October 1.

- Fill out the FAFSA every year. Most people don't bother even though their circumstances change. A sibling starting college might mean more money for you, especially if they're going to an expensive school.

LOAN$

- Every dollar you borrow is going to cost you about $2 by the time you pay the debt. Think about that every time you sip that Caramel Brulee Frappuchino Blended Crème.

- If a grandparent wants to help with tuition, it's best to have them provide a loan rather than cash. (Cash is considered a gift, while a loan at current interest rates doesn't factor in.)

- Federal loans have flexible payment terms if you're unemployed or underemployed. Private loans do not.

$CHOLARSHIP$

- Winning big scholarships is like winning the lottery. Your chances are much better applying to lots of smaller ones.

- Some schools have earlier application deadlines for students who want to be included in the scholarship pool. Know the deadline.

- The amount of work is minimal compared to the potential reward when searching for scholarships. After the first few scholarship applications, the amount of work for each additional application is reduced, since students can reuse and adapt previous application essays.

FINANCIAL AID

- The 'summer melt' happens after May 1 when students change their minds about their 'final' decision and switch to another college. Those students forego their financial aid and scholarship packages, therefore freeing up money for other students. Contact the financial aid office mid-summer and nicely ask if there is any further financial aid that has become available and can be distributed to your financial aid package.

> " I visited the financial aid office during the summer before my freshman year. Classes hadn't started so they weren't swamped yet. It was the best thing I ever did. The adviser took a lot of time with me and got to know my situation. From then on, I always requested him. Over the course of my college career, he saw to it that I got some serious cash. "

Graduate, Biology, University of Michigan
(Been There, Should've Done That—995 tips for making the most of college)

66 I felt like a juggler
trying to keep all the plates spinning.
Because I couldn't decide which
college to go to,
I had to fill out ALL the forms and
keep on top of ALL the deadlines
for ALL of them! 99

Freshman, DePaul U.

you're in!

. . . congratulations!

Your hard work has paid off! But as your high school career winds down and you have one foot out the door, there are still a few things you can do now and through the summer to make your life easier as a college freshman. Your most important assignment: read, study, and scrutinize everything your new school sends you. Along with the necessary forms and deadlines, you'll be notified of all kinds of special freshman programs and opportunities that can make your transition to college a piece of cake. **Take advantage of them.**

Spring:

☐ **Watch** the deadlines for deposits!

☐ **Fill out** necessary forms and return them promptly (housing, roommate profile, medical, etc.). Waiting may affect whether you get into any special programs, your choice of dorms—or even whether you will be able to live in the dorms.

☐ **Read** carefully whatever material is sent to you about freshman programs, activities, and opportunities. You may also check wth the college's web site for a list or call the Department of New Student Services.

☐ **Register** for the earliest orientation session as soon as you're accepted. That should improve your chances of getting the classes you want.

☐ **Request** your housing deposits back from the college(s) you're not attending. If you miss the deadline your money will not be refunded.

☐ **Consider** taking courses at a community college or on your prospective campus during the summer. It's a chance to learn a skill (i.e. time management, computers), brush up on a weak area (i.e. math) or simply get a class out of the way. Find out whether the credits transfer.

☐ **Make sure** that your final transcript is sent to your college.

☐ **Look** for a summer job.

Summer:

☐ **Notify** your college of any scholarships you've received.

☐ **INHALE** your college's website! You'll find anything and everything to get you 'in the loop' academically and socially. Read the the discussion boards and blogs to get 'inside' advice and find anything from books and lofts, to parking spaces. The departmental links are excellent for finding unique opportunities related to a major you may be considering.

☐ **Contact** your roommate. Get acquainted via social media or e-mail and decide who's bringing what. Dorm rooms are small.

☐ **Make a list** of PINS, credit card numbers, registration numbers, and leave them at home where you'll know where to find them. Also, list the serial numbers on computers, printers, bicycles or anything else that may be stolen, so that there's no problem with insurance.

☐ **Check** to see if you can take placement tests online prior to orientation. That could allow you to enroll in courses earlier—and assure your spot in a class.

☐ **Read**. Get a list of titles you'll have to read as a freshman and dig in (page 33).

make the most
of orientation

Orientation is a good time to 'take care of business'. If your school doesn't have a summer orientation, plan a visit anyway so you can:

- **Meet with a Financial Aid Officer.** Summers are a lot more laid back so you'll be able to get advice specific to your circumstances and give him a chance to connect a face with the financial forms... could benefit you in the future.

- **Find a work study job** if you're responsible for securing one.

- **Contact any club**, organization, or activity your interested in. You may be able to jump in sooner and beat the rush for prime positions in the fall.

- **Scan the newspaper** and bulletin boards for lofts, refrigerators, used books, parking spaces, or whatever.

66 I spent a lot of time on my college's website looking at majors and course descriptions before going to orientation. Registration was a breeze because I knew exactly what courses I wanted. 99

Sophomore, Penn State University

too good to miss!

Colleges spend big bucks on programs to help freshmen succeed . . . *but you have to enroll in them!*

Freshman Seminars—Learning Communities— Residential Colleges—FIG's (Freshman Interest Groups)—Mentoring . . .whatever your college calls it, these programs are specifically designed to provide you with a built-in support system of students, faculty and advisers. They allow excellent on-going access to faculty and advisers, and allow you to find your 'niche' academically and socially. *Space is usually limited, so register early.*

Pre-orientation programs. These programs are meant to be nothing more than FUN—an opportunity to bond with fellow freshmen. The activities include such things as wilderness trips, white-water rafting, service projects, retreats, etc. Take a bit of time from your 'last summer' with friends and ease into meeting new ones. Again, space is usually limited so *register early.*

doctor, doctor...

- **Get a physical** in early spring. Schedule vaccinations for: Hepatitus B (3 doses—start in May), Meningitis and Tetanus (if due).
- **Make a list** of your allergies to give to your dorm advisor, especially if you're allergic to medications.
- **Transfer any prescriptions** to a pharmacy near your college.

sticker shock

The first semester can be a quite a surprise for unsuspecting freshmen and their parents. Beyond tuition, prepare yourself for program costs, mandatory fees, incidental fees, and any number of 'add-ons.' Here's the 'real thing'. . .

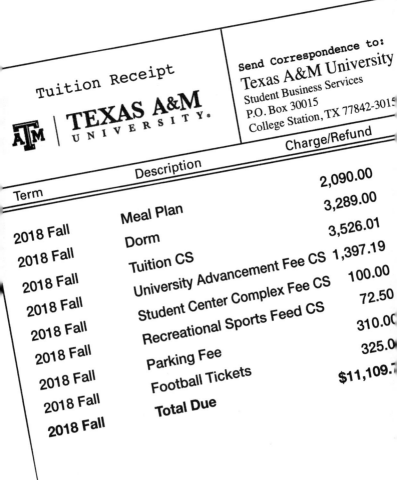

Tuition Receipt

ATM | TEXAS A&M UNIVERSITY.

Send Correspondence to:
Texas A&M University
Student Business Services
P.O. Box 30015
College Station, TX 77842-3015

Term	Description	Charge/Refund
		2,090.00
	Meal Plan	3,289.00
2018 Fall	Dorm	3,526.01
2018 Fall	Tuition CS	
2018 Fall	University Advancement Fee CS	1,397.19
2018 Fall	Student Center Complex Fee CS	100.00
2018 Fall	Recreational Sports Feed CS	72.50
2018 Fall	Parking Fee	310.00
2018 Fall	Football Tickets	325.0
2018 Fall	Total Due	$11,109.7

$$$
dollars & sense

setting up your finances

Along with learning how to say, "Do you give a student discount?" it's time to set up your financial life and familiarize yourself with banking. Talk to your parents now to find out what they expect of you. Have them define what a 'financial emergency' is (hint: it probably won't be new designer clothes for 'rush week') and how it should be handled. Asking them for tips on how to budget your money isn't a bad idea either.

bank that

▷ **If your parents prefer** that you set up an account with their bank, ask for a student account that allows for free checking, no minimum balance, and no ATM or transfer fees.

▷ **Online banks** have lower fees and higher interest. It's basic self-service banking from your computer or mobile. You can track your balance, pay bills, deposit checks remotely, transfer funds and usually there's free checking and ATMs.

▷ **Money is a tough thing to collect from a friend.** There are lots of apps that take the awkwardness out of it by allowing everyone to 'pay up' immediately—Venmo, Square Cash, Apple Pay, Google Wallet—no excuses.

▷ **Use** a bank that has ATMs on your campus, or close by.

66 We do a credit check on
all job applicants before hiring.
It's based on retail accounts, gasoline
cards, rent payments—
but primarily on credit card history. 99

V.P. of Human Resources
*(Been There Should've Done That—995 tips for
making the most of college)*

credit or debit?
the case for/against

Debit Cards:

A great alternative to carrying cash and a safe way to learn about credit without high interest charges. A must-have for the 'self-control-challenged' student.

Going over your balance causes overdraft fees. There's overdraft protection but it has a high interest. No protection if someone steals your card—they've got your cash. Does not build credit history.

Credit Cards:

Can't be beat for real emergencies and if you're responsible, you can build a great credit history. Most cards are theft-protected (if stolen, you don't pay for charges). Look for a card that gives you something back: frequent flyer miles, cash back, and/or purchase protection.

Don't pay off your balance every month and the interest rates will send that balance soaring. There's a chance of graduating with a student loan AND a credit debt. **The real nasty: your future employers check your credit rating.**

To find and compare credit cards, go to:
www.creditcards.com/student/
www.wallethub.com/credit-cards
www.cardratings.com/studentcreditcards.html

tech support

What to buy . . .

Laptop? YES! Check to see if your college or intended major has any specific recommendations or any dictates for software.

Tablet? Maybe. It's easy to carry and the battery life is good. But, it does not replace a computer for things like writing papers and downloading professors' notes.

Smart Phone? A non-negotiable YES! It allows ongoing access to communications from the school, profs, and other students. Price shop—some providers will give you a discount on the phone price, while others will make the monthly payment lower.

Printer? Maybe. They take up space in a small dorm room and most assignments are submitted digitally. But, they're convenient if there isn't access to printing in your dorm, and printer/scanner/copier combos are pretty inexpensive.

Portable phone charger? Yes. They're good to have, especially for long days on campus when you can't get back to your dorm. But they're not cheap. Ask for one as a graduation gift.

Want a deal . . . ?

Consider purchasing your computer and electronic devices directly from your college. Most schools offer students significant discounts, plus you won't have to worry whether your software is compatible with the school's. Another bonus—if your computer needs to be repaired, they may provide a 'loner.'

Avoiding disaster . . .

Don't lose the key! When you buy new software, every package contains a product key that you absolutely need to keep so that if you ever need to reinstall the program, you can. Otherwise, you'll have to buy a whole new program.

▷ **"Apple pickers" beware!** A laptop is stolen every 53 seconds. Apple has a feature called Find My Mac, Find My iPhone, etc.—but you have to turn it on! Software is also available that tracks your computer and even deletes the contents remotely.

▷ **Buy a cable lock . . .** and use it! Even in your own room, and especially at the library. A quick break could be very expensive if your computer isn't attached to something.

▷ **Store it in 'the cloud.'** There are services like DropBox that store your data and it is available to you from anywhere. Another good way to backup is with an external hard drive - you can access it even if the internet isn't available.

insurance
basics

Your possessions should be covered by your parents' home-owners' policy IF you're living in a dorm. If you're living off-campus or planning to move off-campus in your later college years, you'll need your own renter's insurance.

> **Check to see** if there's enough specific coverage on your current homeowners' policy for items such as your computer and jewelry, too. A $1,000 worth of electronic coverage may not be enough if it has to cover both your computer and CD player AND your parents' electronic items. If you have any doubts, talk to your insurance agent about purchasing an additional rider.

> **Find out** if you will still be covered by your parents' car insurance if you're taking your car with you.

> **Don't forget health insurance.** If your parents can't cover you, check with the college for medical and dental policies they may offer.

dollars & sense

☐ **Talk** with your parents. Find out what they will pay for and what you'll be responsible for once you're on campus.

☐ **Set up** your banking with a bank that works best for you. (p. 154) You're looking for convenient ATMs, no fees, no minimum balance, online accessibility and an easy way for your parents to deposit the cash!

☐ **Decide** on a debit or credit or debit/credit card. Research your options thoroughly for the best rates and benefits. (p. 155)

☐ **Get** a taste of reality—find out what the charges are for a bounced check or an overdraft on a debit card. If you know what it costs, you'll be less likely to do it.

☐ **Review** your insurance needs. Ask your parents to check their homeowners' policy to see if your possessions are adequately covered, especially for computers and jewelry. Call your insurance agent if you have any doubt. Colleges offer policies.

☐ **Determine** your computer and software needs and start looking for the best deals—it may be your college that offers it. (p.157)

☐ **Evaluate** your cell phone plan and find out whether your provider has good reception at your new school. You may need to change.

. . . getting ready

Picking out all the things you'll need for your dorm is cool . . . until you realize how all those odds and ends can nickel and dime you to death. Plan ahead, shop wisely and you may even have enough money left over to buy yourself lunch.

> ❝ It's horrible to have to buy toothpaste, shampoo and toilet paper with your own money! ❞
>
> **Freshman, Texas A&M**

what you'll ~~need~~ *want*

Linens:
- 2 sets of twin sheets (long)
- Blankets or quilts
- Pillows
- Mattress pad (long)

Bath:
- Shower shoes, caddie
- Towels
- Soap, shampoo, conditioner
- Toothbrush, paste
- Hairbrush, comb, hairdryer

Desk:
- Stationery (include stamps)
- Calculator
- Calendar, planner
- Bulletin board
- Lap desk

Furniture:
- Full length mirror
- Fold up stools, butterfly chairs, or floor pillows
- Waste basket
- CD player

Storage:
- Bed lifters (creates storage area under bed)
- Storage boxes
- Milk crates, shelves
- Over-the-door rack

Other:
- Lamps, flashlight, batteries
- Sewing kit
- Iron, ironing board
- Dishes, silverware
- Food storage containers
- Wall-friendly poster tape
- Extension cords, surge protectors
- Tool set
- Alarm Clock
- Hangers
- First aid kit
- Ear plugs

To be decided with room-mate:
- Refrigerator/cooler
- Microwave
- Vacuum
- TV

66 You absolutely have to have headphones!
I can jam all night
while everyone's asleep. 99

Sophomore, Miami University

index

index

index

index

index

index

"The problem with college is that you figure it out about the time you're ready to graduate."

-Senior, University of Florida

COLLEGE

4th Edition

Been There
Should've
DONE THAT

995 + tips for making the most of college

★ ★ ★ ★ ★ A Five Time Award Winner!

Collegians across the U.S. tell . . .

- **How to find the best profs**
- **How to choose the 'right' major**
- **G.P.A. 'uppers' and 'downers'**
- **Transfer tips . . . and traps**

Plus

- **The courses you REALLY need
  (according to grads)**
- **How to impress profs
  (according to profs)**
- **What impresses employers
  (according to recruiters)**

*$12.95 US
For educational sales, call
FRONT PORCH PRESS
888-484-1997
www.frontporchpress.net*